Crime Reduction Research Series Paper 9

An Exploratory Evaluation of Restorative Justice Schemes

David Miers, Mike Maguire, Shelagh Goldie, Karen Sharpe, Chris Hale, Ann Netten, Steve Uglow, Katherine Doolin, Angela Hallam, Jill Enterkin and Tim Newburn

The views expressed in this report are those of the authors, not necessarily those of the Home Office (nor do they reflect Government policy).

Editor: Barry Webb
Home Office
Policing and Reducing Crime Unit
Research, Development and Statistics Directorate
Clive House, Petty France
London, SW1H 9HD

Crime Reduction Research Series

This report was commissioned by the Crime and Criminal Justice Unit (CCJU). CCJU is based in the Research, Development and Statistics (RDS) Directorate of the Home Office. The Unit carries out and commissions research on patterns of crime and the administration of justice, to support Home Office aims and develop evidence-based policy and practice.

The Crime Reduction Research Series presents research findings and guidance material relevant to practitioners involved in crime reduction at the local level, and particularly the local crime and disorder partnerships. The series will include work funded under the Government's Crime Reduction Programme as well as other relevant RDS work.

Details of how to obtain further copies of this report can be found on the back cover.

Copies of this publication can be made available in formats accessible to the visually impaired on request.

© Crown Copyright 2001   ISBN 1-84082-692-4
First Published 2001

Foreword

Restorative justice is a topic currently attracting much attention. But there is, as yet, insufficient robust research evidence (from this country at least) on the effects restorative justice has in practice, particularly on reoffending.

We are seeking to address this through our Crime Reduction Programme work on restorative justice. As the first stage of that work, we commissioned this study to evaluate some exisiting RJ schemes. In doing so, the study has produced some very interesting findings on the impacts and cost-effectiveness of restorative justice. It has also provided some important pointers for the next stage of the programme.

David Moxon
Head of Crime and Criminal Justice Unit
Research, Development and Statistics Directorate
Home Office
September 2001

Acknowledgements

We wish to acknowledge the help and assistance of the members of the Home Office Steering Group, especially Pat Dowdeswell and Catriona Mirrlees-Black; the management and staff of the seven schemes we evaluated and of the additional schemes who provided us with details of their work; Jocelyn Kynch, Julie Latreille, Karen Moreton and Tania Intiaz who assisted with data inputting and analysis; Mark Oldfield, Kent Probation Service; Cardiff University Information Services; the anonymous reviewers appointed by the Home Office; and the New Cavendish Club, London.

The authors

David Miers is Professor at Cardiff Law School, University of Cardiff. Mike Maguire is Professor of Criminology and Criminal Justice at the University of Cardiff. Shelagh Goldie is a Research Officer at Goldsmiths College, University of London. Dr Karen Sharpe is a Research Fellow at the Centre for Criminal Justice Studies at the University of Leeds. Professor Chris Hale is the Dean of Social Sciences at the University of Kent at Canterbury. Dr Ann Netten is the Director of the Personal Social Services Research Unit at the University of Kent at Canterbury. Dr Steve Uglow is a Reader In Criminal Justice at the University of Kent at Canterbury. Both Katherine Doolin and Angela Hallam are research students at the University of Kent at Canterbury. Dr Jill Enterkin is a Researcher at the Lord Chancellor's Department and Professor Tim Newburn is Director of the Public Policy Research Unit at Goldsmiths College, University of London.

Executive summary

The aims of the research

This report presents the results of a 15-month study of the effectiveness of restorative justice schemes conducted between July 1999 and November 2000. The principal fieldwork was undertaken between December 1999 and June 2000 in seven restorative justice schemes across England, two of them dealing principally with adult offenders and the other five with juveniles.

The research was commissioned under the Crime Reduction Programme (CRP), a major government-funded initiative aimed at discovering 'what works' in reducing crime and reoffending. The CRP is also concerned to ensure that reductions are delivered efficiently, so a further focus of attention was upon cost-effectiveness in the achievement of the outputs, impacts and outcomes of the schemes examined.

The aims of the research were:

● to identify which elements, or which combination of elements, in restorative justice schemes are most effective in reducing crime and at what cost

● to provide recommendations on the content of, and best practice for, schemes to be mainstreamed.

Research methods

Following an initial feasibility study, fieldwork for the main body of the research commenced in December 1999. The main elements of the fieldwork were as follows:

● the collection of *descriptive information* about the schemes' status, history, philosophy, policies and practices

● the collection and analysis of process and output data about the practical operation of schemes

● the collection and analysis of evidence concerning the impacts of the work of the schemes, short of effects on reconviction rates (see below)

● the collection and analysis of systematic data relevant to measuring the outcomes of restorative justice, in particular any effect that it might have upon reconviction rates

● the collection and analysis of data relevant to the determination of *cost-effectiveness*.

The data collected primarily comprised numbers and types of offences and offenders referred to the schemes, numbers of completed interventions, numbers of victims, interviews with offenders, victims and scheme personnel, estimates of scheme costs, and reconvictions. The fieldwork focused on seven schemes in different parts of England. They were:

- AMENDS (Amends Waltham Forest Victim Offender Mediation Service)
- Gloucestershire Diversion Unit
- Leicestershire Young Offenders Diversion scheme
- Mansfield Restorative Conferencing Programme
- Suffolk County Council (Youth Justice) Caution Plus scheme
- West Midlands Probation Service Victim Offender Unit (Coventry)
- West Yorkshire Victim Offender Units.

Single research visits were also made to six additional schemes during the latter part of the fieldwork. Brief systematic accounts of the activities of each of these schemes are attached as Appendix D.

The research strategy

The research strategy comprised a 'prospective' and a 'retrospective' element.[1] The 'prospective' element of the study included the collection and analysis of descriptive material (mainly documents and records produced by the schemes); the collection and analysis of detailed information about samples of current cases, including cost-related data; interviews with staff members, volunteers, offenders and victims; and the administration of 'CRIMEPICS II' (an instrument to measure changes in offenders' attitudes to crime and victims) to offenders before and after the intervention.

In order to determine the outcomes of restorative justice interventions, a 'retrospective' study was conducted of offenders in respect of whom interventions had been made. This was undertaken in the following two ways:

- a comparison of reconviction rates between offenders who had experienced a restorative justice scheme intervention and control groups of similar offenders who had not
- in the case of the two adult schemes only, comparisons (among both intervention and control groups) between predicted and actual reconviction rates. Predicted reconviction rates were calculated with the use of OGRS 2 and actual reconvictions were determined through the Offenders Index.

---

[1] These elements are more fully described in Chapter 1.

Implementing the research

Carrying out the research proved difficult in a number of respects. As the time-scale was short, the analysis of reconvictions had to be undertaken on retrospectively constructed samples. This meant that reliance had to be placed on schemes' records, which were in many cases fairly sketchy or incomplete. Moreover, some were still quite 'young' and had dealt with relatively few cases. Many schemes operated with few paid staff, relying upon volunteers and a few, key charismatic individuals. The work they were doing was, in most cases, non-statutory; so there was no requirement for offenders (and, of course, victims) to become involved. Finally, one of the adult schemes was almost entirely inactive owing to cuts in resources, while most of the juvenile schemes were severely disrupted by preparations for the introduction of Youth Offending Teams (YOTs) in Spring 2000. These factors combined to make it difficult to achieve intended targets in terms of sample size.

The research analysed the work of the seven schemes under the following headings:

- origins, aims and objectives
- organisation and funding
- staffing and training
- referral criteria and procedures
- types of intervention
- referrals and completions
- current developments.

There was considerable variation in the nature of the schemes' work with victims and offenders. They engaged in activities ranging from, on the one hand, full-scale family group conferences and face-to-face meetings between victims and offenders to, on the other, general 'victim awareness' sessions and initiatives in which offenders write letters of apology. Where contact with victims was not a high priority there are serious doubts as to whether they could reasonably be called restorative justice schemes at all.

Under all these circumstances, pooling data from the various schemes in order to draw general conclusions about the impact or effectiveness of 'restorative justice' was problematic.

Restorative justice interventions: impact on victims and offenders

Interviews with small numbers of victims (23) and offenders (43) indicated that:

- Victims were in general well disposed towards the aims of restorative justice.
- When invited by a scheme representative, victims decided within a day or two whether they wished to participate in its activities.

- Direct mediation between a victim and an offender took place in a very small number of the referrals identified in the research.

- One of the most positive aspects of mediation for victims was the humanising effect of meeting and hearing from, and about, the offender.

- Of those victims who had engaged in mediation, most reported that they had been satisfied or very satisfied with their involvement.

- Where intervention was seen to be most beneficial, the actual process of mediation could take a considerable period of time; it was felt that the length of the process strengthened the overall impact of the service and enhanced its effectiveness.

- Personal letters of apology, which had clearly been written by their offenders and not corrected by the scheme, were well received by victims.

- Victims were disturbed when they were not told of any other purpose to which a letter of apology might be put.

- Both victims and offenders valued mediation sessions that were conducted expeditiously, were responsive to their views, and were concluded with clearly agreed outcomes.

- Offenders welcomed the opportunity to meet their victims and to apologise.

- For offenders engaged in direct mediation, the response of the victim and the victim's family was a key factor in their reaction to the process. Most offenders felt positive about the mediation.

- Most offenders had a positive attitude to the other interventions in which they were engaged.

Restorative justice interventions: outcomes and cost-effectiveness

- The retrospective analysis suggests that interventions by the West Yorkshire scheme had a significant impact on reoffending, both in terms of the offence frequency and offence seriousness.

- No impact was found in the case of interventions by the West Midlands scheme.

- There was no evidence that either of the two 'caution plus' young offender schemes (Leicestershire and Suffolk) had any significant impact on reoffending.

- Although a smaller proportion of the intervention group in the Gloucestershire young offender scheme reoffended within 12 months than in the control group, this was not a statistically significant difference and is accounted for almost entirely by the sex differences in the compositions of the two groups.

- Two features of the West Yorkshire scheme which may be relevant to its comparative success were that firstly, it was made very clear to offenders from the outset that participation would have no bearing on their sentence, and secondly, many of the offenders it dealt with had committed very serious offences and/or were serving long prison sentences.

- Of the two adult schemes, there was evidence that the West Yorkshire scheme was *cost-effective* in reducing further offending. In this scheme the proportion of offenders in the highest risk category that did not reoffend over the subsequent two years was relatively low. In terms of cost per prevented offence the evidence suggests this would appear to be the most cost-effective group to target.

- Information was not available for all of the schemes but the evidence suggests that, while other, unmeasured outcomes may have been achieved, the juvenile schemes as they stood at the time of the study were not cost-effective in terms of reconviction.

- Within the schemes, the involvement of victims (where this occurred) tended to be associated with higher costs. However, the only scheme that routinely involved victims (West Yorkshire) was, for the most part, both lower cost and more effective than the other schemes.

Conclusions

- The schemes evaluated in this research were diverse in their understandings of the notion of 'restorative justice', their degree of focus on victims and offenders, and their implementation of the interventions which they undertook. The schemes were also fragile, being vulnerable to funding cuts, and were often dependent on work 'beyond the call of duty' by small numbers of exceptionally committed individuals.

- Even at the times when they were receiving substantial numbers of referrals, most schemes made unambiguously 'restorative' interventions in relatively few cases. Direct (face to face) mediation was, as a proportion of all the referrals identified, a rare event, and even 'shuttle diplomacy' tended to occur in only a minority of referred cases.

- Whatever its precise form, 'restorative justice' is a labour-intensive and time-consuming activity, beset by communication problems and delays. Particularly where direct mediation is contemplated, it can involve weeks of preparatory and exploratory work, and, even then, many cases do not reach the desired conclusion. This situation raises some doubts about the future potential of mediation as a mainstream service capable of 'processing' large numbers of cases within (or outside) the criminal justice system.

- Victims who had experienced some form of restorative justice were broadly favourable towards the concept. They appreciated the opportunity to "have their say", and some were pleased and even moved to receive letters of apology. Those who had not previously known their offenders often welcomed the provision of information about them, commenting that this gave them peace of mind. About two-thirds believed that the intervention had had some beneficial impact on the offender.

- On the other hand, some victims were sceptical about their offender's motives or found direct personal contact with them unsettling and even intimidating. The most frequently cited negative aspect of involvement with the schemes was the time taken to complete the process.

- The offenders interviewed were generally more content with the intervention in their case than were victims. They appeared to understand the purpose of the intervention and several commented that they welcomed the chance to say sorry. Most had found the experience of meeting their victims embarrassing or upsetting, and in a small number of cases threatening. While the sample was not large enough for full confidence in the results, there were encouraging indications from the 'before and after' scores of the 28 juvenile offenders who completed CRIMEPICS II. These showed substantial improvements in attitudes towards victims and towards offending in general.

- West Yorkshire, the scheme that dealt with the most serious offenders and generated the greatest amount of victim involvement, was the only scheme for which the retrospective study indicated a significant effect on reconviction rates. A sample of adult offenders who took part in direct or indirect mediation did significantly better in terms of reconvictions than a comparable control group. They were also, as a group, convicted significantly less than predicted by OGRS2.

- The other adult offender scheme, West Midlands, did not support this finding, the intervention group doing no better than the control group when account was taken of previous offending. In the case of the three young offender schemes, for which reconviction studies were possible, no significant differences were found between the intervention and control groups in terms of either reconvictions or known reoffending.

- The second principal aim of the research was to provide recommendations on the content of and best practice for schemes to be mainstreamed. The conclusions that we reached were that schemes could benefit from clearer, more systematic, and more developed understandings of a number of key areas of their design and delivery:

  - aims, organisation, staffing and training
  - referral criteria
  - victim and offender protocols
  - interventions
  - closure, follow up and evaluation.

Contents

List of tables

1. Introduction

Background and aims of the research

This report presents the results of a 15-month study of the effectiveness of restorative justice schemes conducted between July 1999 and November 2000. The principal fieldwork was undertaken between December 1999 and June 2000 in seven schemes across England, two of them dealing principally with adult offenders and the other five with juveniles. The research was commissioned under the Crime Reduction Programme (CRP), a major government-funded initiative aimed at discovering 'what works' in reducing crime and reoffending. The CRP is also concerned to ensure that reductions are delivered efficiently, so a further focus of attention was upon cost-effectiveness in the achievement of the outputs, impacts and outcomes of the schemes examined. Equally, as one of the aims of the CRP is to identify effective modes of working that can be 'rolled out' to other areas, the researchers sought to gather examples of best practice from the evaluated schemes and to distil them as general guidelines.

In brief, then, the aims of the research were:

- to identify which elements, or which combination of elements, in restorative justice schemes are most effective in reducing crime and at what cost

- to provide recommendations on the content of, and best practice for, schemes to be mainstreamed.

It should be said at the outset that the research suffered from a number of significant problems. First, as the time-scale was short, the analysis of reconvictions of offenders who had experienced restorative justice had necessarily to be undertaken on retrospectively constructed samples, comprising cases dealt with some years previously. This meant that reliance had to be placed on schemes' records, which were in many cases fairly sketchy or incomplete, both in describing the interventions that had taken place and in providing details of the offenders involved (one scheme, indeed, had already destroyed some of the relevant records). Moreover, three of the schemes dealing with juveniles were still quite 'young' and had dealt with relatively few cases in their first years of operation, so that the number of cases suitable for retrospective analysis was limited.

Secondly, the seven participating schemes were chosen by the Home Office in advance of the research, and by the time the fieldwork began, some important and unforeseen changes had taken place. One of the adult schemes was almost entirely inactive owing to cuts in resources, while most of the juvenile schemes were severely disrupted by preparations for the introduction of Youth Offending Teams (YOTs) in Spring 2000. It had been intended to supplement the retrospective reconviction study with a study of current cases incorporating interviews with substantial numbers of offenders and victims, but for a variety of reasons, including a major downturn in activity in most of the schemes, it proved impossible to reach the target numbers. In the event, we were able to interview only 43 offenders and 23 victims.

Thirdly, none of the schemes was in receipt of any Home Office funding during the period of the study. In addition, some had been the subject of earlier evaluation, prompting an element of 'research fatigue'. Consequently, research requests, particularly those that involved a direct administrative cost (though reimbursement in line with the research budget was offered), were not always favourably received, and co-operation was not always forthcoming.

Finally, while all the schemes claimed to be involved to some extent in 'restorative justice', they had very diverse aims and were engaged in very different kinds of activity. Two, indeed, were essentially 'caution plus' schemes: that is, their main purpose was the diversion of young offenders from court through the provision of a variety of alternative interventions. Although these often included 'victim awareness' sessions, contact between the scheme and victims, let alone arranging 'mediation', was not a high priority and there are serious doubts as to whether they can reasonably be called restorative justice schemes at all.

Research methods

Following an initial feasibility study, fieldwork for the main body of the research commenced in December 1999. The main elements of the fieldwork were as follows:

- The collection of *descriptive information* about the schemes' status, history, philosophy, policies and practices. Here the research was concerned to answer such questions as: how do restorative justice schemes relate to the criminal justice system; what are their basic aims and practices; from where do they get their referrals; what types of offenders do they target and/or exclude; and what are their policies towards and safeguards concerning direct contact with victims?

- The collection and analysis of *process and output data* about the practical operation of schemes, in particular referral and completion rates; the numbers of cases in which particular 'solutions' are reached; and the time taken to process and complete referred cases.

- The collection and analysis of evidence concerning the impacts of the work of the schemes, short of effects on reconviction rates (see below). In the case of offenders, these may include changes in attitudes to crime and/or victims, in behaviour, in levels of employment, or in education attendance. In the case of victims, they may include positive or negative responses to restorative justice initiatives, to offenders and offending, or, more generally, to the criminal justice system.

- The collection and analysis of systematic data relevant to measuring the outcomes of restorative justice, in particular any effect that it might have upon reconviction rates.

● The collection and analysis of data relevant to the determination of *cost-effectiveness*. Here the research sought to: identify the comprehensive opportunity costs of a sample of individuals going through the schemes; identify the costs of alternative disposals; identify and explore causes of variation in costs; link costs directly to outcomes ensuring like is being compared with like; and compare the cost-effectiveness of schemes in achieving desirable outcomes.

The fieldwork focused on seven schemes in different parts of England. They were:

● AMENDS (Amends Waltham Forest Victim Offender Mediation Service)

● Gloucestershire Diversion Unit

● Leicestershire Young Offenders Diversion Scheme

● Mansfield Restorative Conferencing Programme

● Suffolk County Council (Youth Justice) Caution Plus Scheme

● West Midlands Probation Service Victim Offender Unit (Coventry)

● West Yorkshire Victim Offender Units.

Single research visits were also made to six additional schemes during the latter part of the fieldwork. The primary purpose of these visits was to generate further information on scheme management, good practice, intervention strategies and delivery that could be compared with the results of the main survey. Details were obtained by correspondence from a seventh scheme (Sheffield). Brief systematic accounts of the activities of each of these schemes are attached as Appendix D. The schemes were:

● Maidstone Mediation Service

● Milton Keynes Retail Theft Initiative

● Northamptonshire Youth Offending Team and Adult Diversion Unit

● Sandwell Mediation Service

● Sheffield Victim Offender Mediation

● Thames Valley Restorative Cautioning Project

● NCH Marvel Restoration Service (North Wales).

Further details of the research methods used during the fieldwork are provided at appropriate points throughout the text. Here we simply outline the main elements of, in turn, the feasibility study, the prospective analysis and the retrospective analysis.

The feasibility study

Before commencing the fieldwork proper, a three-month feasibility study was conducted, mainly in order to judge whether the data extractable from the schemes' records were adequate for valid and useful retrospective and prospective analyses of the schemes' activities. The principal characteristics of these analyses are described more fully in the following sections. For our purposes, a 'retrospective' analysis could be achieved, first, by a retrospective comparison of reconviction rates between offenders who had experienced a restorative justice intervention and control groups of similar offenders who had not, and second, by a comparison, among those who had experienced restorative justice, between predicted and actual reconviction rates. The 'prospective' study was principally concerned to generate sufficient expenditure data for the purpose of determining the schemes' cost-effectiveness, and sufficient cases for the purpose of interviewing offenders and victims.

Attention was therefore primarily focussed on the information which we would need for the purpose of the analysis of reconviction rates and of cost-effectiveness. The primary criteria that we identified were:

- types of offender
- types of intervention
- the nature of the activity in which the scheme was currently engaged
- the number of referred offenders in selected previous years
- the numbers of offenders being referred during the study timetable
- the lapse of time between the date of referral and the completion of the particular intervention strategy (turnaround)
- the lapse of time between the date of referral and the potential application of any predictive measure of reoffending
- the reliability of the scheme's records
- researcher access to the scheme
- the feasibility of sufficient interviews with offenders and victims.

The overall conclusion was that the records were adequate in most schemes, but that the quality of record keeping was variable and great care would have to be taken in both the collection and interpretation of data. Three schemes (AMENDS, Gloucestershire and Mansfield) were too 'young' to produce substantial numbers of cases in which two years had elapsed since the intervention. For this reason we were unable to include AMENDS and Mansfield in the outcome study, but we were able to conduct a one-year follow-up study in Gloucestershire. There were also concerns about the numbers of cases that would be available for prospective analysis: one scheme (Coventry) was inactive and others were experiencing declines in referrals. Finally, the nature of the interventions varied widely, and it was not even clear that two of the schemes (Leicestershire and Suffolk) could accurately be described as engaged in 'restorative justice'. A more detailed summary of the findings is given at Appendix A.

Prospective analysis

The 'prospective' element of the study included the collection and analysis of descriptive material (mainly documents and records produced by the schemes); the collection and analysis of detailed information about samples of current cases, including cost-related data; interviews with staff members, volunteers, offenders and victims; and the administration of 'CRIMEPICS II' (an instrument to measure changes in offenders' attitudes to crime and victims) to offenders before and after the intervention.

Data were collected systematically on, *inter alia*, the official aims and 'philosophy' of each scheme and each staff's understandings of the aims; the precise nature of the activities in which the scheme was engaged (currently and in the past); numbers of referrals and their outcomes; the types of offences and offenders involved; the time taken to process cases; and the numbers and purposes of visits, letters or telephone calls made.

Interviews were conducted with 27 scheme personnel, 43 offenders and 23 victims. CRIMEPICS II questionnaires were administered by scheme staff to around 45 offenders, but in only 28 cases were these completed both 'before and after' the intervention (which is necessary if change is to be measured).[2] All these totals were disappointing but as noted above, the downturn in the activities of nearly all the schemes meant that there were simply not enough current cases to analyse during the fieldwork period. No 'sampling' was undertaken: details were collected on all current cases, and efforts were made to interview all victims or offenders whose cases were completed.

The researchers also sought to generate data from which the schemes' cost-effectiveness could be evaluated. This involved:

- identifying all the relevant resources (primarily staff, volunteers, and other involved agencies' time) consumed by participants in the schemes for a prospective sample and those retrospective cases where information was available

- estimating detailed unit costs of staff time and key stages in the process for each scheme

- identifying key causes of variation in resources consumed

- using this information to predict the resources consumed by those cases for which information was not available

- identifying the costs of alternatives to the schemes where relevant

- estimating the costs of preventing reoffending where effects are found.

---

[1] Some of the schemes dealing with juvenile offenders were also unconvinced that the instrument was suitable for administration to young people, and declined to co-operate in this aspect of the research.

The assumption underlying this approach was that there would be variation in inputs (i.e. there was not a standard approach adopted for all cases) and that there would be insufficient data on resources used in retrospective records. If there were sufficient information about inputs and/or a standard approach applied then there would be a limited need for a prospective study from the perspective of the cost-effectiveness evaluation. However, a prospective study would only be helpful for predicting costs if there were sufficient similarities between the activities currently being undertaken by the schemes and those undertaken for the retrospective sample. It was also important to be reasonably sure that there would be sufficient numbers of cases available for both prospective and retrospective samples.

Retrospective analysis

In order to determine the outcomes of restorative justice interventions, a 'retrospective' study was conducted of offenders in respect of whom interventions had been made. This was undertaken in the following two ways:

- a comparison of reconviction rates between offenders who had experienced a restorative justice scheme intervention and control groups of similar offenders who had not

- in the case of the two adult schemes only, comparisons (among both intervention and control groups) between predicted and actual reconviction rates. Predicted reconviction rates were calculated with the use of OGRS 2 and actual reconvictions were determined through the Offenders Index.[3]

In the two adult schemes, the control groups were constructed from cases referred to the schemes over the relevant period, in which no further action was taken. In the case of West Yorkshire, by far the most common reason for this was that the victim failed to respond or declined to become involved. Reasons for 'no further action' were less clear in the West Midlands, but at least 28 per cent of cases were discontinued owing to the withdrawal of the offender after sentencing. West Midlands accepted referrals pre-sentence and although no intervention took place at that stage, the offender's willingness to participate was brought to the court's attention. It is likely therefore that some offenders agreed to the referral in the hope of a reduced sentence, losing interest once the court case was over. In West Yorkshire, by contrast, offenders had no prospects of benefiting in this way. Comments on the possible implications of this difference will be made in the course of the analysis in Chapter 5.

In the three juvenile schemes in which outcome analyses were conducted, control groups were constructed either from cases which had been referred to the scheme but where no intervention had occurred (Leicestershire and Suffolk), or from cases taken from years prior to the establishment of the scheme (Gloucestershire).

---

[3] The Offender Group Reconviction Scale (OGRS) is based on an offender's gender and age at sentence plus variables derived from previous and current criminal justice history: number of previous convictions; type of offence; age at first offence; rate at which offender has acquired convictions and number of previous custodial sentences while under the age of 21. For more details see Copas and Marshall (1998). The Offenders Index is the main source of data on adult offenders' reconvictions. The normal follow-up period is two years. It is updated quarterly, six months in arrears. This means that it is normally only possible to obtain information on reconviction rates passing through programmes after a three-year period has elapsed.

Structure of the report

Chapter 2 provides a review of recent literature and legislation on restorative justice. Chapter 3 comprises a summative and comparative analysis of the work of the seven schemes evaluated in the study. Chapter 4 examines the impact of the interventions on victims and offenders, while Chapter 5 focuses on the specific outcome of reconvictions. Chapter 6 focuses on the issue of costs and cost-effectiveness. Chapter 7 draws some broad conclusions and presents a number of recommendations drawn from the study.

The appendices cover: (A) a summary of findings of the feasibility study; (B) more detailed scheme descriptions; (C) additional cost-effectiveness data; (D) an account of practices in the seven additional schemes; (E) copies of the research instruments; and (F) the bibliography.

2.　　Restorative justice: definitions, theory and practice

Introduction

This chapter seeks to update Marshall's comprehensive overview (1999) of the meanings, purposes, practices and impacts of restorative justice. In broad and simple terms, 'restorative justice' signifies those measures that are designed to give victims of crime an opportunity to tell the offender about the impact of the offending on them and their families, and to encourage offenders to accept responsibility for, and to repair, the harm they caused. Its general aims are to reduce reoffending, to restore the relationship between the victim and the offender that was disturbed by the offence, and to improve victims' experiences with the criminal justice system.

Marshall's paper repeatedly draws attention to the pluralistic nature of the many restorative justice initiatives currently being practised in Great Britain, Australasia and North America. "Restorative justice is not, therefore, a single academic theory of crime or justice, but represents, in a more or less eclectic way, the accretion of actual experience in working successfully with particular crime problems" (1999, p.7). The diversity of practice, the powerful sense of ownership on the part of its practitioners, the tensions between offender-centred and victim-centred criminal justice and penal policies, divisions as to its theoretical base, and what counts as success, are all matters that continue to exercise those who have, in the short time since Marshall's review, contributed to the restorative justice debate.[4]

The literature should also be seen in a wider context of concern for the place of the victim in the planning and implementation of new criminal justice policies, both at a general level (Sanders, 1999; Crawford and Goodey, 2000; Walgrave, 2000), and in respect of such particular initiatives within England and Wales as the *Victim's Charter* (Hoyle, Morgan and Sanders, 1999), victim impact statements (Hoyle et al., 1998), and victim contact work with the probation service (Crawford and Enterkin, 2000). Of prime importance are the United Nations *Declaration of Basic Principles on the use of Restorative Justice Programmes in Criminal Matters* published in draft in October 1999, and Recommendation No. R(99)19, Mediation in Penal Matters adopted by the Council of Europe in September 1999.

The chapter is divided into three parts: theory, practice and evaluation. Particular mention is made of the recent statutory initiatives contained in the Crime and Disorder Act 1998 and the Youth Justice and Criminal Evidence Act 1999.

---

[4] Amongst other publications, this debate has been conducted in a number of thematic journal issues; for example, Western Criminology Review (Jackson, 1998), Criminologie (Jaccoud and Walgrave, 1999); and the International Review of Victimology (Griffiths and Bazemore, 1999).

Theory

Recurring paradigms

The primary elements of restorative justice are, perhaps, uncontroversial, even though they may be stated in different ways. As a convenient shorthand expression, it commonly applies (Dignan, 2000b; p. 296) "to a variety of practices which seek to respond to crime in a more constructive way than is conventionally achieved through punishment. At the risk of over-simplification, the philosophy on which it is based can most helpfully be summarised in terms of the 'three Rs' of Responsibility, Restoration and Reintegration." Its more particular purposes include the prevention of reoffending, the recognition of the victim's interest in the amelioration of and acceptance by the offender of the harm done, and of the community's interest in the longer term rehabilitation of and support for the offender, and a reduction in criminal justice costs.

But there are also differences in how these elements might be described (Weitekamp, 1999b; p.1). As the Council of Europe notes (1999, p.17), "in the United Kingdom, 'mediation' and 'reparation' were originally used interchangeably and now there is a growing tendency to refer more generally to 'restorative justice'." In other European countries the distinction persists between mediation as a technique of conflict resolution which, in addition to many other contexts, has applications to offending behaviour, and reparation or restoration, which connote responses within a more limited criminal justice environment.

As two almost simultaneously published statements by the Council of Europe and the United Nations underline, there continue to be ideological, as well as terminological, differences about how the subject matter is to be defined. Of primary significance is the question whether the restoration of the victim by the offender *necessarily* requires the intervention of a non-criminal justice third party. An 'impartial third party' is a constitutive element in the Council of Europe's Recommendation No. R(99)19 *(Mediation in Penal Matters)*, which defines mediation as "a process whereby the victim and the offender can be enabled, voluntarily, to participate actively in the resolution of matters arising from the crime through the help of an impartial third party or mediator. The reference only to the victim and the offender as parties does not exclude other persons (legal and physical) participating in the mediation." By contrast, this element occupies only a contingent place in the United Nations *Draft Declaration on Basic Principles on the Use of Restorative Justice Programmes in Criminal Matters* (1999). This defines restorative justice as a process "in which the victim, the offender and/or any other individuals or community members affected by a crime participate actively together in the resolution of matters arising from the crime, often with the help of a fair and impartial third party". For many, it is precisely the traditional criminal justice agencies which need to be disengaged if the victim, the offender and the community are to recapture and resolve the conflict (which may include recapturing the entire criminal justice system; Wright, 1999).

However, as Bazemore (1999) has commented, even for those who subscribe to a victim-centred approach, an honest answer to the question, 'what's in it for victims?' would be that restorative justice should not be viewed as a panacea (1999; p.315). "It is no substitute for an active and aggressive victims' movement and, like current 'victims rights' philosophies, is no substitute for individual victims and advocacy groups monitoring and questioning whether policies and practices implemented in their name in fact serve their interest." In short, restorative justice ideologies are as much about political action as they are about responses to offending behaviour (New Zealand Ministry of Justice, 1999).

There are also differences as to whose interests are to be preferred where only some of the objectives of the process can be realised. For example, Marshall (1999; p. 5) identifies the following common international use of the phrase, restorative justice: *"a process whereby parties with a stake in a specific offence collectively resolve how to deal with the aftermath of the offence and its implications for the future"*. This stresses the shared interests of all its stakeholders (Braithwaite, 1999), yet an equally common understanding is that the ideological purpose of the restorative justice paradigm, in direct contrast with retributive or rehabilitative responses to offending behaviour, is to place the victim at the centre of the process (Presser and Lowenkamp, 1999). These differences are clearly of relevance, for example, to the choice of criteria for evaluating the success of restorative justice initiatives.

Still others question whether the theoretical backbone of restorative justice is sufficiently well articulated to warrant the repeated references to its constituting a paradigm shift in criminal justice (Bazemore, 1998; Bazemore and Walgrave, 1999; Weitekamp, 1999a; Young, 1999). Meier (1998), for example, addresses the sceptics' position, that restorative justice compromises principles of equality (not all offenders are treated the same for the same offence), neglects the public interest in prosecution and punishment, and disregards procedural rights, by a reworking of the definition identified by Marshall, as follows (1999; p.137): "restorative justice is the process whereby the offender voluntarily and autonomously accepts his or her responsibility for the offence and eliminates the consequences by positive and social-constructive activities". While this reworking also addresses a major shortcoming of the standard procedural definition, the exclusion of victimless crime, Meier argues that it seems more appropriate simply to describe restorative justice as a new perspective on criminal justice, rather than to engage in the "euphoria" of talk about new paradigms.

New legislative initiatives

The White Paper, *No More Excuses – A New Approach to Tackling Youth Crime in England and Wales* (Home Office, 1997), led to the introduction in the Crime and Disorder Act 1998 and the Youth Justice and Criminal Evidence Act 1999 of a number of new measures concerning the youth justice system.

First, sections 65 and 66 of the Crime and Disorder Act 1998 introduced a new procedure for the reprimand and warning of children and young persons which replaces the police caution. In essence, these represent a tiered response to first time offending: a reprimand is intended for young offenders who have not previously been in trouble, a warning for those who have. Young offenders who receive warnings will be referred to a youth offending team (YOT). Also introduced by the 1998 Act, and which came into operation on 1 April 2000, YOTs operate under the auspices of the local authority. Their purpose is to agree, co-ordinate and monitor programmes of behaviour for young offenders. These may include rehabilitation programmes, which may in turn include sessions on victim awareness or the wider consequences of offending behaviour.

Second, there are new orders applicable to young offenders who come before the court. 'Referral orders', introduced by section 1 of the Youth Justice and Criminal Evidence Act 1999, are mandatory for most young offenders pleading guilty at their first court appearance. The court must refer them to a youth offender panel established by the local YOT. In this case the statutorily stated aim of the programme of behaviour is to prevent reoffending; the means to be guided by the principles of restorative justice. Whatever is agreed is confirmed in a youth offender contract. Section 8(2) provides an indication of what restorative practices may be included in the contract: direct and indirect reparation, mediation with the victim, participation in initiatives such as alcohol or drug awareness programmes. In her review, Ball's misgivings concerning referral orders stem largely from managerial concerns. The apparent simplicity of the procedure (2000; p.212) "belies at a practical level the controversial aspects of the mandatory order, the possibility of confusion at the interface between court and panel, the potential for panels to be overwhelmed by the number of orders, uncertainties about the membership and powers of panels, and the flawed nature of the so-called 'contract' based on a 'programme of behaviour' made between the offender and the panel". Her concern about the confused ideology underlying the procedure makes the same point as pervades Marshall's overview: "the order is founded on a 'cherry-picked' eclectic mix of principles and philosophical approaches".[5]

Where the trial proceeds and the young offender is convicted, section 69 of the 1998 Act permits the court to make an 'action plan order' with a view to securing his/her rehabilitation, or preventing the commission of further offences. This is a "community order" within the meaning of the Criminal Justice Act 1991, which means that it must be 'serious enough' to warrant a community sentence. Under the action plan, the offender may be required to make reparation to "the community at large" or to 'a victim of the offence or person otherwise affected by it' who consents to the reparation being made.[6] Exactly the same requirement may be imposed under a 'reparation order', introduced by sections 67 and 68 of the 1998 Act and applicable upon conviction in cases where the court concludes that the offence is not so serious as to warrant a community sentence. Even so, the court is required to set the reparation requirements at a level 'commensurate with the seriousness of the offence'. Reparation orders

---

[5] Referral orders are currently being piloted and evaluated in 11 areas across England and Wales. National implementation is scheduled for April 2002.

[6] This option has also been added to the requirements that may be imposed under a supervision order (section 71 of the 1998 Act).

are by no means a novelty within the court's sentencing options;[7] this is, however, the first occasion on which they have been extended to young offenders. The Home Office envisages that reparation may involve "writing a letter of apology, apologising to the victim in person, cleaning graffiti or repairing criminal damage". (Home Office, 1997; para. 4.14). Neither are these outputs novel; apologies in particular have figured in virtually all of the schemes reviewed during our research.

Reactions to this initiative have been mixed. Wasik (1999) has raised concerns relating to the identification of victims, for example, in the robbery of a small store owned by a large trading company. The Act requires the court to identify a 'person' as a victim of the offence: this clearly includes the counter-staff, and might also extend to the company's representative. Also present were an elderly customer who suffered shock and a young child who was put in fear by the imitation firearm that was used; later the child's parents were distressed to hear what has happened. These are all persons 'otherwise affected' by the offence. However, the Home Office guidance, that the reparation should "relate as closely as possible to the offence itself", does not wholly answer the connected questions; to which victims should the court give priority in the making of a reparation order, and to what extent should it take account of the offender's interests.

This tension is also identified by Morris and Gelsthorpe (2000) who question whether reparation orders, when combined with the other changes introduced in 1998 and completed in the 1999 Act, can as Dignan (1999) suggests, be seen to situate "some elements of the restorative approach as part of the *mainstream response* to offending behaviour by young people". To the contrary, they argue (and this is reminiscent of Davis et al.'s critique (1988) of the early victim/offender mediation projects) that the continued focus on blaming and punishing will subvert the White Paper's restorative aspirations. Morris and Gelsthorpe conclude (2000; p. 29): "It is likely that restorative practices will develop in a somewhat ad hoc fashion at numerous decision points in the youth justice system, but at no point will the key participants in all of this – the offenders, victims and their families or support – actually be able to take charge. Victims will no longer be marginalised in quite the same way that they are currently, but their involvement will hardly be significant. Offenders may be coerced into reparation. Nothing in the research literature suggests that this will be likely to reduce reoffending".

Practice

Models

Whatever the theoretical justification for restorative justice, there is also, as there are terminological differences at the international level, a plethora of descriptors for the varying practices that claim to fall within its ambit. Informal mediation, victim-offender mediation, victim-offender conferencing, victim-offender groups, family group conferencing, restorative

---

[7] Limited powers were available to the court under section 11 of the Criminal Justice Act 1948 and were expanded in the form of compensation orders under the Criminal Justice Act 1972, re-enacted as sections 25-38 of the Powers of Criminal Courts Act 1973. These have themselves been re-enacted as sections 130-4 of the Powers of Criminal Courts (Sentencing) Act 2000.

conferencing, restorative cautions and community conferencing are only the most common names used in England and Wales. Other jurisdictions feature sentencing circles, tribal or village moots, community panels or courts, healing circles and other communitarian associations (Braithwaite, 1999). These discrepant usages have prompted some writers to propose some definitional rigour (Liebmann, 1999), but as Marshall (1999, p.27) noted, programme organisers typically display a strong sense of ownership for their preferred methods, which may translate into a reluctance to be dictated to by a central authority.

The development of mediation models across Europe is, as the Council of Europe described them (1999, pp.10-11), uneven, "and in most instances it is still at its initial stages." The preferred models are themselves diverse (Weitekamp, 1999b; pp.3-4); indeed, some practitioners argue that therein lies their strength: it is for the community that wishes to introduce restorative justice to choose the model that best suits its characteristics (Wright, 1998).

Likewise, descriptions of restorative justice practice (of whatever type) vary considerably in scope, aspiration and style. Some, in particular those written by practitioners, tend both to report on a particular project or initiative, and to use any claimed success to reaffirm the central values of this approach in preference to other, more traditional responses. Within England and Wales, this combination is literally exemplified by Pollard's account of the Thames Valley Police Restorative Justice Initiative, "Restoring the faith" (1999; see also Pollard, 2000; Walker 1999).[8]

Implementation protocols

While practice may vary, the literature discloses significant uniformity about a number of matters concerning the conduct of the intervention, procedures for victim and offender contact, training and evaluation. At the international level, for example, these figure as standards within the Appendix to the Council of Europe's Recommendation (1999) and in sections II-V of the United Nations' Principles (1999) (see also The Crime Prevention Council in Denmark (1999)), and at the local level, in the Thames Valley Police's *Facilitator Training Manual* (1999) and, both by prescription and example, in the many training guides produced by Mediation UK (1999).[8]

Evaluation

Restorative justice interventions have been evaluated in a variety of ways. Some of the most common are victims' satisfaction with the process and any consequential changes in their perception of and willingness to assist the police and the criminal justice system more broadly; reduction in reoffending and attitudinal change in offenders; and reduced costs for the police, the courts and post-sentence agencies. The results of the research reviewed by Marshall show varying levels of success as measured in these and other terms. Evaluations by victims, offenders and community representatives tend to show high levels of satisfaction with the

---

[8] The Chief Constable of the Thames Valley Police, Charles Pollard, has been responsible for the dissemination of 'restorative conferencing' for young offenders, as an alternative to their being processed through the courts. The first of its restorative justice schemes was established in 1995 as a youth crime group in Milton Keynes (a recent evaluation is Mackie and Burrows, 1999), later extended to the Milton Keynes Retail Theft Initiative (see Appendix D for brief descriptions of both schemes).

process. Rigorous valuations of reoffending are few in number. Those that exist typically show a small positive effect, though sample sizes, at least in England and Wales, have been small.

Reviewing international research findings, Weitekamp (1999b; pp.12-13) concluded that while victim-offender mediation and restorative justice models appear sound in theory, their evaluations suffer from a number of shortcomings. These include: the unsystematic application of restorative justice models and programmes; a disproportionately high number of juvenile, first time and property offenders; poor planning, unsystematic implementation and short-term evaluations.

As in the past, empirical research both illustrates and questions these difficulties. Three recent studies of small societies found their communitarian practices "vibrant and resilient" (Banks, 1999; p.401; see also Elechi, 1999; Zellerer, 1999). The disputes under review largely concerned theft, minor personal violence and breaches of domestic arrangements. By contrast, Umbreit et al. (1999) challenge the assumption that restorative justice practices are inapplicable to serious personal victimisation. They report on Canadian initiatives in which victims of sexual assault and attempted murder (and the victim's family in the case of murder) are increasingly seeking and successfully completing restorative meetings with the offender. When sensitively handled, "it is clear that the principles of restorative justice can be applied in selected cases of severe violence" (1999; p.340). Against the high levels of victim satisfaction indicated by preliminary data, they are quick to caution against over-enthusiastic application. The authors also draw attention to a sequence of unanswered questions, including the definition of 'severe violence' and the selection criteria to be applied to the victims, offenders, families and others who might claim an interest in the process. They conclude (1999; p.340) that "far more rigorous longitudinal, qualitative and quantitative studies are clearly needed in this emerging area that holds the potential for exceptionally high positive impact on participating parties while also including significant risks as well". These need to focus (Weitekamp, 1999b; Umbreit et al., 1999; Griffiths, 1999) on such matters as best practice, natural experiments, large-scale re-offending data, and long-term effects on both victims and offenders.

A study of reintegrative shaming in Canberra (Sherman et al., 1999) was able to report positively on the experiment's posited outcomes, but others have remarked on the difficulties that attend the introduction of pilot projects which are dependent on police or court referrals. Bazemore (1999) noted the barriers created by court culture and protocols in the United States, while in their review of a Queensland legislative initiative permitting victim-offender community conferencing, Prenzler and Hayes (1999) found that the pilot successfully delivered many key restorative justice outcomes, but that victims' opportunities to benefit from reparation were seriously compromised by the low level of police referrals and the total absence of court referrals.

Prenzler and Hayes' work built on an earlier study of the same pilot scheme, which likewise showed very high levels of victim satisfaction, but because no reliable reoffending data were available, could say nothing about its impact on recidivism (Palk et al., 1998; see also Linden and Clairmont, 1998; Jackson, 1998). And, as Griffiths (1999; p. 293)) noted, while community conferencing holds "considerable promise as a more effective way in which to address the needs and concerns of crime victims, their families, and communities, … there has been no systematic study of the extent to which restorative/community justice effectively addresses the needs of crime victims, reduces vulnerability to future victimisation, and decreases the marginality that victims often experience."

Within England and Wales, the results of the current evaluation of the Thames Valley initiative being conducted by the Centre for Criminological Research, Oxford University will not be known until the research concludes in 2001. In the meantime, those responsible for its implementation are persuaded that it works. This is so, Pollard urges, even if conferencing does not lead to reductions in reoffending. Conferencing "is still immensely valuable in view of all the qualitative benefits it brings to the criminal justice process – particularly to victims, offenders and their families". (Pollard, 1999; p.38). Others are less sanguine, remarking on the care that needs to be taken not to pressurise or exaggerate the benefits to the victim (George, 1999). Other recent evaluations likewise suggest caution, if only for the reason that some of the schemes that have been researched have themselves been sorely hampered in delivery by resourcing and other constraints (Crow, 1999). Even for those where there is statutory funding, managerial and administrative inefficiencies may obscure effective delivery, thus subverting evaluation in terms of the scheme's restorative justice objectives (Dignan, 2000a; 2000b).

3.   The seven schemes

Introduction

This chapter comprises a summative and comparative analysis of the activities of the seven schemes, organised under the following headings:

- origins, aims and objectives
- organisation and funding
- staffing and training
- referral criteria and procedures
- types of intervention
- referrals and completions
- current developments.

Each of the sections below contains a table summarising the activities discussed under that section's headings. A more detailed description of each scheme may be found in Appendix B.

Origins, aims and objectives

Three of the schemes included in this research have their origins in the 1980s. West Yorkshire and the West Midlands, which have dealt with both adult and young offenders, were two of the four original Home Office funded experimental reparation projects which began work in

Table 1. Origins, aims and objectives

Scheme	Start year	Offenders	Orientation[9]
AMENDS	1997	young	mixed
Gloucestershire	1997	young	mixed
Leicestershire	1985	young	offender (caution plus)
Mansfield	1998	young	offender
Suffolk	1992	young	offender (caution plus)
West Midlands	1985	young adult	mixed
West Yorkshire	1985	young adult	mixed

[9] By 'orientation' we mean the predominant focus of the scheme's aims and objectives. A scheme would be victim orientated whose primary objective is to give victims of crime an opportunity to tell the offender about the impact of the offending on them and their families; it is offender orientated if its primary objective is to encourage offenders to accept responsibility for, and to repair, the harm they caused. Some - mixed - schemes seek both objectives.

1985. Those in Leicestershire (1985) and Suffolk (1992) were caution plus schemes for young offenders only. The other three schemes, which also deal only with young offenders, are of more recent origin: 1997 (AMENDS, Gloucestershire) and 1998 (Mansfield).

In some, aims and objectives were clearly articulated in private and public documents and were routinely disseminated to their staff, and to the victims and offenders with whom they dealt. Others displayed less clarity, for example, substituting procedures for aims and objectives, requiring inferences about them to be drawn from external police or probation documents, or failing to deliver a consistent message to their staff, with resulting confusion as to what counts as a successful intervention.

The schemes' aims and objectives were of two main types: those with a primarily offender-oriented approach, and those which sought to place equal emphasis on the victim and the offender. The West Yorkshire scheme, for example, saw the process of mediation as providing victims and offenders with the opportunity to resolve conflicts, "within the wider context of the criminal justice system". Similarly, AMENDS, which dealt only with young offenders, sought "to offer help to victims of crime to understand what has happened to them; and to help offenders understand and take responsibility for their actions". By contrast, the Leicestershire caution plus scheme emphasised the development of "clear and consistent cautioning, diversion and prosecution criteria which emphasise the nature of the offence, the characteristics and antecedents of the offender and which take account of the effect of offending on victims as well as public interest factors."

They also varied in their understanding of what might be meant by 'restorative justice'. Measured against Marshall's formulation of the phrase as "a process whereby parties with a stake in a specific offence collectively resolve how to deal with the aftermath of the offence and its implications for the future" (1999; p. 5), there was considerable variation in the schemes' intervention practices. These variations are of importance when we come to measure success.

Organisation and funding

Six of the schemes have been funded directly by one or more core agencies, major contributions coming from the probation service, social services and the police, or from a combination of these sources. In some instances a range of independent grant-making trusts and charities has supplemented their funding. There was also substantial indirect funding in the form of continuing salary payments to professional staff seconded to the schemes. This was particularly the case in Mansfield, which has no dedicated funding but is almost entirely supported by police staff resources. In the case of the juvenile schemes now subsumed within the YOT arrangements, funding will be delivered and managed by social services.

Table 2. Organisation and funding

Scheme	Primary (P) and secondary (S) funding				Organisation (lead agency)
	Police	LA	Probation	Other	
AMENDS		P		S	A (charity)
Gloucestershire	P	P		S	M (social services)
Leicestershire	P	P	P		M (police)
Mansfield	P				A (police)
Suffolk		P			A (social services)
West Midlands			P		A (probation)
West Yorkshire			P		A (probation)

Notes
Funding: Where P appears more than once as primary funding, there is approximately equal funding from each. LA: local authority. Other: independent grant-making trusts and charities.
Organisation: A = single-agency; M = multi-agency.

Some of the schemes have experienced difficulties as their funding agencies have assumed other priorities. Likewise payments from charity and other private sources are vulnerable to other demands, and even where such funding does continue, it is dependent on the schemes' fund-raising efforts, which themselves represent a resource use.

Their organisation largely reflected the schemes' funding arrangements. Where there was a single funding agency, the scheme was physically located within one or more of its premises, depending on the number of areas covered, and was answerable directly to it, typically via a senior agency representative or a small committee. In the case of the West Midlands and West Yorkshire these were drawn from the probation service; in Suffolk, from the social services. At area level a more junior representative, assisted by a salaried co-ordinator, supervised level daily operations. In the absence of direct funding, Mansfield appeared to have no coherent or effective management structure; responsibility for the implementation and development of the scheme had simply been added to the existing workload of three police officers.

In the case of the multi-agency arrangements in Gloucestershire and Leicestershire, the hierarchical structure was similar, but at both the supervisory and management levels there was necessarily a greater number of members. Teams comprising senior representatives from all the partner agencies oversaw the scheme's overall operation; below that, a multi-disciplinary management team had responsibility for the scheme's routine operation, the intervention team itself being led by a co-ordinator who was a member of the management team. Because they need to reflect the interests of all their stakeholders, the organisational hierarchy of multi-agency arrangements may well be disproportionate both to the level of funding and the scope of the scheme's activities, possibly to the detriment of focused and effective service delivery. By contrast, AMENDS was formally independent of its funding agencies. While its management committee comprised individuals drawn from those and other community agencies, their position as trustees meant that they acted in a private capacity. Like other schemes, AMENDS' daily management was in the hands of a paid co-ordinator.

It should be noted that since Spring 2000, the organisation of the schemes dealing with juvenile offenders has been subsumed within the YOT arrangements, although in most cases the committee structures have remained largely intact.

Staffing and training

Two broad distinctions may be made concerning the schemes' staffing arrangements. First, there were those staff who were responsible for some aspect of a scheme's administration, alongside whom were those who actually dealt with offenders and victims. In some instances, an individual might perform both roles. The second distinction is between those who were employed by the scheme, and those who gave their time voluntarily. Schemes' reliance on the latter group varied considerably. Both distinctions have implications for the level and intensity of staff training, which was variable.

All but one of the schemes employed at least one person full-time to manage their day-to-day implementation. Often designated as 'co-ordinators', their tasks included logging referrals, assessment and allocation of casework, training and supervision of mediators and reporting to the scheme's management committee. All schemes also employed, either full or part-time, secretarial or other support staff to assist with routine administration. The number of co-ordinators and support staff in any one scheme varied, reflecting such factors as its funding levels and the expansion or contraction in its activities.

The co-ordinators' backgrounds varied. Where they were salaried, some had been seconded from or had experience of similar work with adult or juvenile offenders in another branch of social services, in the police, or in the voluntary sector; some co-ordinators had qualifications in or experience of mediation or family group work. In other cases, no particular background of this kind was evident, beyond the co-ordinator's professional knowledge of the criminal justice system.

Those who actually dealt with offenders and victims were variously designated as 'facilitators' or 'mediators'. Although not all the schemes offered mediation as an intervention, we will use that shorthand here. As in the case of the co-ordinators, the experiential background of the salaried mediators varied, and some were employed only on a sessional basis, as the number of referrals warranted. The primary additional factor in this context was the use of volunteers. Two schemes relied very heavily on volunteers, one less so, and four not at all.

Table 3. Staffing and training

Scheme	Employed mediators	Volunteer Input	Training	
			Initial	Continuing
AMENDS	agency	substantial	4 days	policy
Gloucestershire	seconded	none	3 days	needs driven
Leicestershire	agency (police)	substantial	4 days	policy
Mansfield	agency (police)	none	7 days	policy
Suffolk	agency (social services; YOT)	none	minimal	needs driven
West Midlands	agency (probation)	none	minimal	
West Yorkshire	recruited	limited	3 days	variable

Volunteer mediators were not expected to have any particular experience in dealing with offenders or victims, nor were formal qualifications required. They came from all walks of life, a minimum age of 18 being invariably applied. Some had themselves been victimised in the past; others, indeed, had been offenders. Police checks were routine.

Both newly-employed staff and volunteers underwent initial training. This varied between three, four and seven days, provided either by the scheme's own experienced staff or by experts contracted for the purpose. In some schemes, this also figured as part of the application and vetting process,[10] arguably an expensive use of scheme resources where an applicant is rejected.

The most developed training programmes dealt with such matters as the value, role and practice of mediation, the youth justice system, restorative justice and the scheme's own referral and administrative processes. In some cases, the training led to a formal accreditation. Further training was available in most schemes, though in some instances this tended to be needs driven rather than the deliberate working out of a staff development policy. A primary characteristic was that training frequently took place 'on the job', and newcomers were typically required to 'shadow' an experienced mediator before they were given a case of their own. Some had introduced a formalised support and monitoring system for their volunteers. The practice of shadowing, which varied in its application both within and between the schemes, also applied to some salaried mediators.

Whether as volunteer or salaried mediators, those who had received training appreciated it, but a number of those who were interviewed said that they would have valued more focussed training. Some of the co-ordinators and the mediators were themselves sufficiently well qualified or experienced to deliver training both to their own and to other schemes.

---

[10] The Thames Valley Restorative Justice Initiative was a popular choice (see Appendix D).

Referral criteria and procedures

Five of the schemes by definition dealt only with young offenders. Their intervention point was immediately post-arrest or at first court appearance, in all cases coupled with a guilty plea. These are characteristic features of 'caution plus' and other diversionary policies. It was not uncommon for some offenders to be referred who had been cautioned on a previous occasion. Offences referred included minor incidents of criminal damage, theft (in particular, shop theft), handling stolen goods, burglary, assault and taking a vehicle without consent. Some offences were specifically excluded; for example, homicide, racially or sexually motivated offences, domestic violence, aggravated assaults and robbery, drugs offences and possession of offensive weapons.

While the other two schemes, West Midlands and West Yorkshire, have dealt with young offenders, our focus in their case was only on their adult referrals. As might be expected, these produced some much more serious offences. Even so, and reflecting the young offender schemes, West Yorkshire tended to exclude rape and other sexual offences and to exercise caution in cases of domestic violence and in racially motivated offences. A significant difference between these two schemes was that in West Yorkshire, the offender's willingness to participate in mediation was deliberately not brought to the court's attention before sentencing. In West Midlands, by contrast, it was included in pre-sentence reports, often with the express purpose of achieving a reduction in sentence.

Table 4. Referral criteria and procedures

Scheme	Intervention point	Offences (excluded)	Criteria for participation	
			Offender	Victim
AMENDS	post arrest	minor P, A (sex, race)	G; W; C; H	W, S, I
Gloucestershire	post arrest	minor P	G, W, H	W, I
Leicestershire	post arrest (caution plus)	minor P, A	G, W, I, F	not applicable
Mansfield	post arrest)	minor P, A	G, W, I	W, I
Suffolk	post arrest (caution plus)	minor P, A	G, W, H	not applicable
West Midlands	pre-sentence	P, V	G, W, I	W, I
West Yorkshire	pre- and post-sentence	P, V (sex, race)	G, W, I	W, S, I

Notes
A: assault
C: signs of contrition or remorse
F: other factors affecting the offender
G: guilty plea or other admission
H: home visit in presence of young person's parents
I: pre-intervention interview
P: property offences (typically theft, criminal damage, taking a vehicle without consent)
S: safety of both parties in intervention
V: violence against the person
W: willingness to participate

Referrals to the schemes came from a variety of sources. In the 'adult' schemes, these included the police, probation, CPS, courts and, occasionally, Victim Support. In the schemes dealing with young offenders, most referrals came from multi-agency panels, to which the police had referred the offender,

On receiving referrals, schemes applied a variety of criteria designed to assess the offender's and, where they sought such engagement, the victim's suitability for intervention. In the case of those schemes which were primarily offender-oriented, victim-related criteria were under-developed, even if there was occasional contact with victims. Depending on the scheme's organisational status, offender-related criteria were to be found in police diversion manuals, or in its own practice handbook. These criteria stated such formal prerequisites as an admission of guilt, residence within the scheme's area (reflecting both resourcing and jurisdictional considerations) and a willingness to participate in intervention, possibly coupled with some expression of remorse. Other factors included the gravity of the offence, previous offending, the offender's response to any previous interventions, and any other relevant domestic circumstances.

A young offender's suitability for intervention would be determined initially as a paper exercise by the scheme's co-ordinator, an employed mediator or by a multi-agency referral panel such as a juvenile liaison committee or similar body. This was followed by a direct personal assessment made by the co-ordinator or other scheme representative in the presence of the offender's parents or guardians. The mediator alone would visit adult offenders. Assuming the offender's suitability at this stage, further action typically required scheme approval. Where the proposed intervention was intended as a diversion measure and approval was not forthcoming, the offender would be simply cautioned or, possibly, prosecuted.

Where approval was given the victim would be contacted, but only where it was clear that the offender wished to meet, to make reparation or in some other way to apologise. This wish assumes the victim's identification. This was particularly an issue in shop theft, where the victim could well be conceived as being its legal owner or manager, rather than the counter staff. While some mediators expressed reservations in interview, proxy or representative victims figured in a number of schemes' practices. On the other hand, one of the branches of the West Yorkshire scheme did not deal with offences against large commercial ventures. As with offenders, a residence requirement in the case of 'natural' victims, and a willingness to participate were standard criteria. Where direct mediation was a possibility, the participants' safety was a criterion common to all schemes. The victim's wish not to be involved in direct mediation was final.

Types of intervention

Previously we remarked, with reference to Marshall's (1999) formulation of the phrase 'restorative justice', on the schemes' differing aims and objectives. If we recall also that restorative justice is defined in the United Nations Draft Declaration (1999), as a process "in which the victim, the offender and/or any other individuals or community members affected by a crime participate actively together in the resolution of matters arising from the crime, often with the help of a fair and impartial third party", we can say that between them, the schemes engaged in work representing all its primary forms (albeit, as will be shown later in a minority of the cases referred to them).

Table 5. Primary types of intervention

Scheme	DM	IM	FGC	Apology	DR	IR	VA	O
AMENDS	Y	Y		written, spoken	Y			
Gloucestershire	Y	Y	Y	young	Y			
Leicestershire				young		Y	Y	Y
Mansfield			Y	young	Y			
Suffolk				young		Y	Y	Y
West Midlands	Y	Y		young adult	Y			
West Yorkshire	Y	Y		young adult	Y	Y		

Notes
DM: direct mediation
IM: indirect mediation
FGC: family (or restorative) group conferencing
DR: direct reparation or compensation to the victim
IR: indirect reparation
VA: victim awareness
O: other offender intervention (anger management, careers advice, substance abuse advice)

Given their centrality to analysis of restorative justice, it is useful to amplify aspects of these headings. In *direct* and *indirect* mediation the victim and the offender are helped by a facilitator to communicate with each other. Direct mediation comprises face-to-face contact between victim and offender (and, where a juvenile, the offender's parent or guardian), together with a trained mediator. In the case of indirect mediation there is no personal contact between victim and offender; instead the facilitator sees each party separately and helps them to voice their feelings about the offence. Messages can be conveyed in a variety of ways that include relayed spoken apologies and letters. *Family (or restorative) group conferencing* comprises a meeting between the victim (or a representative), the victim's family or other supporters, the offender, members of the offender's extended family, and representatives of the justice agencies. All parties are invited to put their point of view about the offending behaviour and its consequences. These conferences are often based on the notion of reintegrative shaming.[11] *Direct reparation* can be taken to include financial compensation to, rather than work-in-kind for, the victim. *Indirect reparation* is in essence work designed to benefit the community.

---

[11] See Braithwaite (1989); Morris and Maxwell (2000); Young (2000).

Direct mediation occurred in a very small proportion of referrals, though as one might expect, it figured more prominently in those schemes exhibiting a primarily victim-oriented approach. Indirect mediation, particularly in the form of letters of apology, was much more common, although some of the more offender-oriented schemes attached little importance to their delivery.

Indeed, the latter schemes – in particular, Leicestershire and Suffolk – tended to make contact with victims in only a small minority of cases. Their main priority was to confront the offending behaviour of the young people referred to them. Their interventions consequently devoted attention to a whole range of issues, of which understanding of the impact of their offending on victims was only one. These included the offender's explanation for the offending; its impact on family relationships; general victim awareness; substance abuse awareness; future behaviour; and personal goals such as education and work.

Procedure

The content of the intervention would be arranged in advance. Where victims were involved in either direct or indirect mediation, the schemes employed elaborate procedures for ensuring that they were aware of what was to happen, and were fully consenting, in particular to face-to-face meetings with the offender. This was also the case with family group conferences. Indirect reparation was in essence work designed to benefit the community.

Direct mediation followed the established format in which each party speaks without interruption about the offence and the impact it has caused, responds to the other, asking questions and providing information, and makes a closing statement. In the case of indirect mediation, having visited each party in turn relaying each other's views, the mediator negotiated an outcome to which both parties consented.

A primary outcome of direct mediation was a direct apology, but both direct and indirect mediation might also result in victim or community reparation. While the victim's views on reparation (or, indeed, any other disposal) were sought, they were not determinative of the final outcome. Another common outcome was a relayed oral or written apology. Letters of apology would be sent via the scheme, which might also scrutinise them lest they revictimise the victim.

Some schemes engaged in mediation concluded the process with a later visit to the victim, a debriefing of both parties, the completion of an evaluation form, or a letter to the offender, for the broad purpose of self- and scheme reflection. Mainly for reasons of lack of time and resources, these events did not always occur.

Venue

Direct mediation always took place at a neutral venue. This practice is generally accepted as being conducive to victim safety and the generation of positive outcomes. The need for a neutral venue was felt to be less strong in the case of retail theft initiatives, where the victim was a representative of the retail sector; in these instances, the meeting might well take place at the shop in question.

Where there was no direct victim-offender contact, individual sessions with the offender might take place at the office, the young person's home, at school, or in some public place such as a cafe. Group sessions, for example with a prison officer, might also be arranged.

Referrals and completions

Table 6 summarises the number of referrals made during specified referral periods, together with their outcomes. The referral periods shown differ because we could not identify any one period for which the schemes were all able to supply comparable statistics. It should also be emphasised that their records were not always sufficiently detailed and accurate in their descriptions of interventions to permit exact counting. Accordingly, the figures given are approximations.

Table 6. Referrals and completions

Scheme	Referral period	Referral numbers	DM	IM	Other	Outcome unknown
AMENDS	04/98-04/00	328	7	26	34	261[12]
Gloucestershire	11/97-10/98	144	27	55	38[13]	24
Leicestershire	01/94-12/99	2,502	0	150[14]	1,358[15]	994
Mansfield	07/98-04/00	132	17	17[16]	86	12
Suffolk (South)	01/95-12/96	663	0	5[17]	133	525[18]
West Midlands	01/96-12/97	166[19]	5	8	79	74
West Yorkshire	10/99-04/00	350	10	89	0	241[20]

[12] The majority of referrals were of young offenders who had been reprimanded or given a final warning; the records did not show what further action might have been taken.

[13] All 38 cases involved victim awareness work with the offender.

[14] This is an estimate of cases in which the offender wrote a letter of apology to the victim. It is not possible to determine the exact number from the scheme's records.

[15] Comprising Panel Cautions and cases in which the young offender agreed to some form of offender-centred intervention.

[16] These cases mainly involved a restorative caution in which the offender wrote a letter of apology to the victim. It is not possible to determine the exact number from the scheme's records.

[17] While the practice of writing letters of apology was not unknown in South Suffolk, the numbers were very small. It is not possible to determine the exact number from the scheme's records.

[18] The total of 663 is the number of young offenders referred to the Youth Liaison Committee. Of these, 138 were referred and accepted for caution plus, and 98 were completed. The remainder (525) were prosecuted, dealt with as simple cautions or no further action. As explained in the text, data for the other two Suffolk divisions were unreliable.

[19] Adult offenders only referred at the Crown Court or by magistrates. The 79 "Other interventions" were cases in which the offender was seen once or twice for the purpose of writing a pre-sentence report; a number of these meetings would have included victim awareness. The 74 cases in the 'unknown' category were no further action.

[20] This figure includes 95 referrals which led to an assessment of the offender, but which, for various reasons (primarily participant unwillingness or unsuitability) did not proceed to mediation. Some of the remaining 146 may constitute cases in process or pending, but no figures were available for these stages.

Outcomes are presented as:

- 'DM': direct mediation; face to face mediation, retail theft initiatives, restorative or family group conferences
- 'IM': indirect mediation; shuttle mediation, letters of apology, reparation or compensation to the victim
- 'other': other intervention; other work with offenders, which may or may not include 'victim awareness' work
- 'outcome unknown': which may include no further action or cases where figures are unavailable or too imprecise for firm allocation to another category.

For the reasons outlined in Chapter 1, limited and/or reduced resources constituted a major obstacle to the successful promotion of interventions for all the schemes. In the case of the five which dealt only with cases involving juvenile offenders, the position was exacerbated by the introduction of YOTs in early 2000; in most cases their level of activity prior to this date had been greatly reduced owing to staff training and other preparations for the change.

In West Yorkshire, other factors, such as the victim's unwillingness, the pressure of statutory work, the amount of time involved in setting up meetings, and the fact that quite a high proportion of referred offenders were serving prison sentences were additional reasons why the number of direct mediations which took place during the research period amounted to only 10 cases out of 350 referrals.

In the case of the West Midlands, referral practice was fraught with problems in the late 1990s. A real lack of resources prompted the probation management to instruct its officers not to make referrals, notwithstanding their suitability. Also, because the purpose of the offender indicating a willingness to be involved with mediation was to record that fact in a report to the court, a reduction in sentence was seen as an end in itself. As a consequence, many offenders dropped out once they had been sentenced. As human resources declined, the years between 1995 and 1997 saw an increase in the proportion of referrals in which no action was taken, equilibrium in the proportion of reports written, and a decrease in the number of offenders seen more than once. By early 1998, the West Midlands scheme had all but ceased work.

Their recent commencement was an additional factor affecting completion rates in the case of three of the young offender schemes. In its first two years April 1998-2000, AMENDS received 328 referrals, leading to 67 interventions (seven direct mediations, 18 letters of apology, eight relayed spoken apologies, and 34 visits to offenders' homes). In 80 per cent of referrals, therefore, there was no further action. This is largely accounted for by the fact that for most of this period, the scheme had only one paid part-time staff member and 11 volunteers, many of who were inexperienced at victim offender mediation and required the co-ordinator to accompany them on home visits and mediation work.

Restorative justice intervention in Mansfield was of a similar order, at around 25 per cent of referrals. Between July 1998 and April 2000, 132 offenders were referred, but only 17 restorative conferences, which are attended by a victim, were completed. The vast majority of the remaining referrals led to a 'restorative caution', a process very similar to the old-style of police cautioning.[21] During this period, there were two major hiatuses in Mansfield's activities caused by staffing problems, the more serious of them between December 1999 and March 2000 (the period of our prospective research), when there were only 10 referrals to the scheme.

By contrast, the more securely funded Gloucestershire scheme was able to undertake direct or indirect mediation in well over half of 144 referrals received in its first year.

Between 1995 and 1999, the number of offenders referred annually in Leicestershire declined from 540 to 274. While an increasing proportion of referred cases had received Panel Cautions, still only half of those referred were dealt with in this way, and half of the referred young people agreed to undertake work with a volunteer. There were no reliable data available on dropout rates, but a review of the scheme's completed intervention files gave the impression that the majority of offenders completed the intervention.

The incomplete Suffolk records, supported by staff interviews, allow us to estimate that approximately 20 to 25 per cent of cases resulted in a recommendation for caution plus. Of these, at least two-thirds completed the process.

Current developments

In the case of the schemes dealing only with young offenders, the most significant development during the research period was their preparation for the implementation of YOTs. As we noted, its immediate impact was to divert their attention and, consequently, their resources, to this recently imposed statutory burden. Now that they are in operation, some of the schemes have been revitalised. Referrals have expanded both in quantity and in offence range, new staff have been appointed, and existing staff have either been the recipients or the providers of training about the Final Warning programme. Work practices have changed to reflect the referral and assessment procedures, and the time limits for offender contact and case assessment. Apart from these externally driven changes, one scheme has developed its own initiatives, building on its existing mediation practices and staff safety protocols.

Developments in the two schemes that also deal with adult offenders are mixed. West Yorkshire announced in June 2000 that victim-offender mediation work was to have a reduced priority in order that it could comply with its Victim's Charter obligations. Although the West Midlands scheme was operating at a very low key at the time of our fieldwork, a new mediator is now to be appointed.

---

[21] That is, a short transaction in which the offender admits guilt in exchange for not being prosecuted. The admission remains on the police files for five years. If the offender commits no further offence during this time, the file is cleared.

Conclusions

What are we to conclude from the history of these seven schemes? Perhaps the clearest message concerns the variability and changeability of both their practices and their fortunes. Under the malleable rubric of 'restorative justice' they have engaged in activities ranging from, on the one hand, full-scale family group conferences and face-to-face meetings between victims and offenders to, on the other, general 'victim awareness' sessions and initiatives in which offenders write letters of apology which may never be delivered. Equally important, they have operated in a quickly changing political environment, which has been only intermittently supportive of restorative justice initiatives and in which funding has been short-term and unreliable. As a consequence many have had to operate with few paid staff, and have had to rely upon volunteers and a few, key charismatic individuals. Moreover, the work they have been doing is, in most cases, non-statutory; there has been no requirement for offenders (and, of course, victims) to become involved.

Perhaps predictably, therefore, the seven schemes being evaluated were at differing stages of development: some in decline, others apparently undergoing reinvigoration. Partly this was a result of statutory changes affecting youth justice, partly just a consequence of the funding and staffing issues mentioned above. Under these circumstances, pooling data from the various schemes in order to draw general conclusions about the impact or effectiveness of 'restorative justice' is problematic. Although such an approach is forced upon us in some parts of the analysis by insufficient numbers of local cases (see next section), when it comes to the main analysis of outcomes in Chapter 5, we shall consider each scheme individually.

4.   Impact

Victim impact

Three of the seven pre-selected research sites had little or no contact with victims during the fieldwork period. The West Midlands-based scheme had been receiving very few referrals for some time before the research began. Those in Leicestershire and Suffolk were long established diversion schemes which, whilst seeking generally to address the victim's perspective in their work with offenders, rarely made contact with individual victims or involved them directly in the process. We therefore conducted interviews with victims from only four of the schemes: AMENDS, Gloucestershire, Mansfield and West Yorkshire.

Our original intention was to interview around 100 victims, but owing to the general downturn in the schemes' level of activity (see Chapter 1) and practical difficulties in setting up interviews, this proved impossible. We set out to interview as many victims as possible from cases which had involved some form of contact with these schemes and which were completed during our main fieldwork period (i.e. between December 1999 and June 2000). The schemes were asked to contact all such victims on our behalf and to pass on a request for interview. However, the process of making contact, securing agreement and arranging interviews was both very difficult and prolonged. In the end, interviews were achieved with a total of 23 victims. The small sample size, together with its possible unrepresentativeness (see below), makes it difficult to generalise the victims' responses. Their individual views remain, however, important.

Indeed, it is difficult to put a precise figure on the total number of relevant cases dealt with by the four schemes over the six months, as their records were not always clear. The records suggest that around 45 cases of 'direct' mediation and 150 of 'indirect' mediation (mainly letters of apology sent to victims) took place during the period. However, many of these cases had still not been 'closed' by the end of our fieldwork period, so we were unable to interview the victim. Moreover, busy scheme members were often tardy – and in some cases reluctant – in making efforts to contact victims on our behalf. It should also be noted that many of the 'victims' were businesses, where there was no obvious individual, in the sense of having been personally victimised, to interview.

Victim profile

While not necessarily representative of all victims, the 23 who were eventually interviewed covered a fairly wide range of types of case. The group included five representatives of victimised businesses and 18 individual victims (see Table 7). Among the latter, interviews were conducted with nine men and nine women. The youngest victim interviewed was 13, and the oldest, 72 years of age. The mean age of the sample was 45. However, all 18 of the individual victims described themselves as being of 'white British' ethnic origin. This homogeneity was surprising given the ethnic diversity of the populations of both West Yorkshire and the Waltham Forest district of London served by AMENDS. It is not possible to say whether the ethnic minority victims in these areas are less likely to use their schemes' services, or whether their absence from this group was an artefact of the small sample size or the difficulties in arranging interviews. It is unsurprising that none of the victims believed that the crimes committed against them had been racially motivated.

Table 7. Number and type of victims interviewed during the research, by scheme

Victims	Schemes				Total
	AMENDS	Gloucestershire	Mansfield	West Yorkshire	
Individual	1	2	5	10	18
Business	4	0	1	0	5
Total	5	2	6	10	23

A majority of the individual victims said they had not known their assailant prior to the commission of the crime. Of the seven victims who did have previous knowledge of their offender, one was a relation, two described the offender as a 'friend' and the others as either an 'acquaintance' or a 'neighbour'. When asked whether they had been the victim of a crime on any previous occasion, the majority said that they had not.

The offences and their impact on victims

Nearly half of the crimes that had been committed against the interviewed victims were acquisitive in nature, predominantly burglary, theft and shoplifting. Just over a quarter were violent offences or had resulted in serious personal injury to the victim (manslaughter, death by dangerous driving, GBH and common assault). The remainder included several instances of criminal damage, a public order offence and arson (see Table 8 for detail). The most serious offences were associated with the West Yorkshire scheme,[22] which dealt mostly with adult offenders: half of those interviewed had burgled and the four cases of serious personal violence or injury in the sample came from this scheme. The majority of the business victims included in the sample (four of the five) were dealt with by AMENDS. The small sample size does not, however, allow us to draw any conclusions about typical victim profiles within the schemes.

---

[22] These included: one manslaughter, one death by dangerous driving, one GBH and one drunk driving incident in which the victim had to be hospitalised for several weeks as a result of the incident.

Table 8. Types of crimes committed against the victims interviewed

Type of offence	Frequency[2]
Burglary	6
Shoplifting	4
Theft/handling	2
Criminal damage	4
Common assault	3
GBH	1
Death by dangerous driving	1
Manslaughter	1
Drunk driving (causing serious personal injury)	1
Arson	1
Public Order Offence	1
Total	**25**

A slight majority of those interviewed said that the crime had affected them "very much". About a quarter had been affected "quite a lot", the remainder only "a little" (see Table 9). None said that the crime had affected them "not at all". This response might be expected from those victims who had become involved in the work of such schemes; conversely, it is reasonable to assume that victims for whom the crime had had little or no impact would be less likely to do so. There were ethical difficulties associated with obtaining from most schemes the confidential details of victims who had refused involvement with them. In the rare instances where this had been possible, victims either did not respond to the researcher's attempts to make contact or did not wish to participate in the study.

Table 9. The extent to which victims said they were affected by the crime

Type of victim	Extent to which victim was affected by the crime				Total
	Very much	Quite a lot	A little	Not at all	
Individual	9	5	4	0	18 (78%)
Business	4	1	0	0	5 (22%)
Total	13 (57%)	6 (26%)	4 (17%)	0 (0%)	23 (100%)

While the victims of serious personal violence were all affected "very much", there were no obvious associations between types of crime or of victim and the extent to which victims were affected by their experiences. The 'large business' victims, all of who had suffered a shoplifting offence, said that they had been affected "very much" by the crime. Usually they related this

---

[23] Total exceeds the number of victims interviewed as one victim experienced multiple offences.

to their company's broader experience of theft and to the cumulative and persistent influence of shoplifting on business rather than the impact of the specific case which had brought them into contact with the scheme.

Contact with the schemes

In almost all cases, contact with victims had been initiated by the scheme. There were only two instances of the victims themselves (or their friends/family) seeking out the scheme. Several of the business victims felt that the local mediation scheme should increase its profile so as to encourage more of a two-way referral process, but it was not clear how they envisaged such an arrangement operating or being regulated.

A cold-call visit either to the victim's home (six cases) or the victimised retail outlet (two cases) was the initial mode of contact in almost two-fifths of cases. Otherwise, telephone calls accounted for a third of first contacts, a letter was sent in a quarter of cases and the remainder could not recall how contact had been made.

When first approached by a scheme representative, most of the victims were able to decide about their participation quite quickly. Nearly a half of those interviewed decided immediately and just under a quarter needed only a day or two. Three needed a week or more to decide.[24] It seemed possible that the mode of initial contact and service delivery might be influencing acceptance rates but the data were insufficient to allow this to be determined here.

Victims' perceptions of the schemes

Most of the victims seemed to hold traditional views about the delivery of criminal justice; few had been aware of the existence of locally established restorative alternatives. Nonetheless, they displayed both an open-mindedness about what one victim described as "one of those American ideas", and a willingness to become involved even when, as in a few cases, victims said they had not clearly understood what was entailed or expected of them. As the victims in the sample had not been interviewed prior to their involvement in the scheme, it is not possible to compare their pre-intervention expectations with their post-intervention experiences.

Victims were offered the different types of interventions identified in Chapter 3:

- direct and indirect mediation
- family (or restorative) group conferencing
- direct and indirect reparation.

Regardless of the type of intervention, victims regarded the intervention in which they had participated as "a good idea", "good in principle" or "good in theory". However, the majority then went on to express quite ambivalent views both in terms of their experience of the schemes' procedures and their outcomes.

---

[24] The rest could not recall how long it had taken them to decide.

Victims' responses to the schemes' initial approach varied between scepticism, enthusiasm, apprehension and curiosity. In cases where the intervention was an alternative to some other form of disposal, some felt that the offender was "getting off lightly", viewing the process as a "soft" option. However, several victims found the existence of such schemes encouraging, expressing their concern about the treatment and welfare of the offender, especially in the cases of juveniles and young adults. Some had been willing to take part in a scheme because they believed that in so doing they would keep the offender from prosecution and from acquiring a criminal record.

(a) The purpose of interventions

While a few victims appreciated the opportunity provided by the scheme simply to "have their say", many others were cautious about the offender's motives in co-operating with restorative programmes. They were willing to be conciliatory, but were equally concerned that they should not be taken in by the offender's disingenuous behaviour, the aim of which was to secure a favourable sentence.

These concerns proved well founded in the case of one victim who had entered into mediation with the offender. Describing herself as "unemotional" about the burglary and damage to her home, and being more concerned for the welfare of the imprisoned offender, she had written a reassuring reply to a "genuine" letter of apology she had received from him. She described her anger upon discovering the subsequent use of her letter during a court hearing in the offender's defence. The subversion of the objectives of mediation in this case raises serious questions about the measures in place within schemes for protecting victims and ensuring that they are clearly informed of likely outcomes and the use of the information they provide.

Victims were particularly attentive to the tone of offenders' communications, whether made indirectly or during face-to-face meetings. In relying on them to assess whether the offender seemed "genuine" or not, letters seemed to hold the greatest potential for leaving victims circumspect. Victims generally appreciated sincere, personal letters which had been clearly penned by the offender. Echoing the sentiments of several others, one described feeling "very touched" by the gesture. However, the well-intentioned intervention of adults in the writing efforts of young offenders was unhelpful. Victims did not appreciate the practice of tidying up the presentation of letters, for example by typing out hand-written notes and correcting spelling errors.

(b) The format of interventions

Victims generally agreed that they had felt listened to, treated respectfully and allowed to have their say "most of the time" during the interventions. However, their misgivings were reinforced by procedures both in some mediation sessions and in the conferencing format. On occasions these were felt to be unresponsive to their position and were perceived as unduly formulaic. One victim, describing her direct mediation session with the offender as "very structured", commented that throughout she had wondered, "why am I here, who is this for?" Another described the session as "very structured and too regimented – we were told when we could speak". During some conferences, victims seemed to feel that they were doing little more than going through the motions, as some offenders, seemingly barely able to understand the process or comprehend what was required of them, had been "fed answers". Making a similar point, another victim considered the option of attending the large gathering of a conference to be "a big fuss" over what she felt was a relatively minor offence, better dealt with by other means. She opted not to attend the conference feeling sure that she would only feel "embarrassed" and "very silly".

Offers of reparation work or payment of compensation seemed particularly problematic. Victims were disappointed by unfulfilled agreements or, as in one case, insulted at the suggestion that the offender, who had damaged her property, be "let loose" on her garden.

(c) Revictimisation

Direct mediation was felt to be particularly relevant to those who had known their assailants. Four such victims expressed this view, even though two of them were, in the event, disappointed by the mediation in their cases. While it appears to offer the opportunity for more meaningful interaction between victim and offender than the 'shaming' platform of the restorative conference, mediation is a daunting experience for some victims. The most frequently cited negative aspect of involvement with the schemes was the time taken by the whole process. This was particularly relevant to mediation, which one victim described as "taking four to five weeks" just to set up, and another said had taken, "months and months when we wanted answers straight away".

In some instances victims found intimidating the circumstances under which the mediation meetings had taken place. The close relative of a victim killed by his partner described going to the offender's home for the mediation as "terrifying". In another case the victim was disturbed by the experience of meeting the offender in prison, commenting that he would have been happier to receive a letter from him. These two cases involved very serious crimes, which no doubt contributed to the victims' apprehension, but there is also the suggestion in the second that the victim perceived that the scheme had pushed him into going to the prison. Whether or not there is any substance in this particular suggestion, some victims seem to have found themselves submitting to what could have been foreseen as potentially traumatising experiences.

(d) A source of information

Victims who had not previously known their offenders generally seemed interested in the schemes' services as a means of receiving personal information about them. In particular, they wanted to understand the offender's motivations for the crime. Two of the most frequently cited positive aspects of their involvement were, first, the peace of mind derived from obtaining such information, and second, the humanising effect of meeting the offender.

There were also requests for "more information" or "more feedback", especially in response to questions about improvements to the schemes' future operations. They were made, for example, in respect of those schemes that had inadequate or seemingly non-existent mechanisms for closing cases. Victims who had contributed complained that they had been left, as one put it, "high and dry", never having been informed of the offender's reaction to their input. In other instances, requests for information about the offender might be regarded as intrusive. For example, some victims (often the large businesses), having, as one said, put in "a lot of effort on this" wanted to know whether "it worked?". Requests for longer-term access to details of the offender's behaviour, in particular, reoffending, requires schemes to address the delicate balance between providing victims with reasonable information and ensuring that offenders' rights and privacy are protected.

(e) Restorative impact

Two-thirds of victims felt that the intervention had made an impact on the offender, but opinion was more evenly divided on the question whether the offender had made sufficient amends for the offence: just over a third agreed, but over half thought not. A burglary victim who had taken part in what for her was an otherwise satisfactory mediation session, and who had accepted reparation from the offender, later commented, "He has not made up, he can't pay back what he did".

These responses suggest that victims are not necessarily persuaded by a scheme's avowed restorative aims and principles, but instead derive benefits, and measure their satisfaction, from its other aspects (for example, as a provider of information). Over two-thirds of the victims reported that, overall, they had been either "satisfied" or "very satisfied" with their involvement in the scheme and less than one in five said that they were either "dissatisfied" or "very dissatisfied".

Offender impact

Analysis of offender interviews

Interviews were completed with 43 offenders in total, from six of the seven sites; AMENDS (eight interviews), Gloucestershire (six), Leicestershire (five), Mansfield (six), Suffolk (15), and West Yorkshire (three). There was little activity in the West Midlands-based service.

Of the 43 offenders interviewed, 37 were male and six were female. All were young offenders except for the three from West Yorkshire who were adults in their 20s. The youngest offender interviewed was 12 years and the oldest was 26 years. The mean age of the sample was 15.6 years. Three-quarters of offenders interviewed described themselves as being of "White British" ethnic origin. Other ethnic groups represented were Pakistani, Mixed Race and Black British. As with the victim interviews, the small sample and lack of representativeness makes it impossible to generalise the offenders' responses.

The most common offence committed was shoplifting (one in five), followed by theft/handling, criminal damage and taking without consent.

Table 10. Types of offences committed by the offenders interviewed

Offence	Frequency	Percentage
TWOC[25]	4	9
Theft/handling	6	14
Theft/shoplifting	8	19
Burglary (OTD)[26]	3	7
Burglary (dwelling)	3	7
Criminal damage	6	14
Common assault	1	2
ABH	2	5
Robbery	1	2
Arson	3	7
Other	6	14
Total	43	100

Thirty-nine of the 40 young offenders received a caution for the offence, the other a supervision order. All three adult offenders received custodial sentences of between 18 and 48 months for offences of domestic burglary and street robbery. Most of the offenders interviewed (27) did not know their victims (12 of these were individual victims and 15 were commercial or local authority bodies). Of the offenders who had previous knowledge of their victim, three were related to the victim, two described the victim as a friend and five were either a neighbour or acquaintance.[27]

Offenders' contact with the schemes

About two-thirds of offenders were told about the scheme by the police. In most of the remaining cases, their Youth Offending Team, probation officer or the scheme itself informed offenders of the programmes. The offenders were offered different interventions including one or more of the following:

● a preliminary interview with a scheme worker

● two or more sessions with a scheme worker

● group work

● reparation or financial compensation for the victim

● reparation for the community

[25] Taking a vehicle without consent.

[26] Burglary of commercial premises.

[27] Out of the remaining six offences, four were for possession of drugs and two were classed as 'other' in the interview schedule.

- a letter of apology to the victim

- the opportunity to meet or communicate indirectly with the victim

- attendance at a restorative group conference.

One scheme offered the offender referral to other programmes.

Many of the offenders could not recall how they felt about what they were offered but some spoke of feeling "anxious", "nervous" and "not knowing what to expect" before taking part. Many thought that they would be "shouted at", "lectured at" and "judged" and were surprised and pleased when this was not the case. Those who were given the opportunity to write a letter of apology to their victim or meet them in person often preferred the former option as it "seemed less scary". A few offenders were pleased to be given the chance to meet their victim and say sorry "so that things could be finished and they could move on".

Twenty-six of the 40 young offenders interviewed took part in some type of diversion activity, which normally consisted of a number of sessions with a scheme worker or volunteer. A few of these cases also included work or financial compensation for the victim, work for the community, writing a letter of apology or meeting the victim.

The other 14 young offenders did not take part in any formal diversion activity but nevertheless had meeting(s) with a scheme worker that resulted in a letter of apology to the victim and/or meeting with the victim or a restorative conference. Two of the adult offenders wrote a letter of apology and one met the victim.

Offenders' perceptions of the schemes

Most of the offenders appeared to understand why they were involved with the scheme and what it was trying to achieve with them. Those undertaking diversion activities thought that they were intended help "keep them out of trouble", "stop them offending", and were their "one last chance". Most were very aware that if they offended again then they would be going to court. Some also spoke of being helped to recognise and understand the impact of their offending on others, not only their victims. Some of those involved in mediation work or who attended a restorative conference spoke of the chance to say sorry and to make up for what they had done. As one offender said, "it makes you realise what you do affects other people and gives you a chance to apologise".

Generally, most offenders felt that their participation had turned out to be much less stressful than they had expected, and they had mainly positive reactions to their involvement. In response to prompted questions,[28] more than four in five, regardless of the form of intervention in which they participated, felt listened to, allowed to have their say and claimed to be treated respectfully "all or most of the time". The personality and approach of the scheme representative and the response of the victim (where applicable) seemed to be key elements

---

[28] See Offender's Interview Schedule, Appendix E, section 4, qq. 10-15.

in whether the offender responded positively to the process and engaged in the intervention.

Offenders from both diversion and more mediation/conference-based schemes, stressed that "someone spent some quality time with me", "listened to me", "didn't judge me" and "respected me". Others, especially those who took part in a diversion programme, spoke of the practical help they received, such as helping them get back into school, getting them employment or a place on a training course. One offender spoke of the amount of time that the scheme worker spent with him filling out training application forms and taking him to an interview. Others spoke of how the scheme helped build and repair relationships with their parent(s). One offender said, "my parents never understood me, now we get on like a house on fire".

Although most offenders were generally positive, there were some that thought the process "was a waste of my time", "boring" or "silly." One who took part in a diversion programme felt that the scheme worker was "stirring up" issues and then leaving her and not helping her sort them out. She spoke of wanting to reoffend in order to get caught and go to court instead of having to complete the sessions. Notably, in a few cases the process seems to have had negative consequences, including an offender who was "picked on" and victimised by the victim and the victim's family after the conference they both attended. Also, one offender spoke of his mother who "cried all the time and could not sleep" because of the way the scheme had treated the incident and, in the offender's view, tried to "stir up things" between the victim's and offender's families.

(a) Attitudes to offending

Four in five of the offenders felt that taking part in the scheme had helped them to understand that what they did was wrong. Many indicated that while they knew, at the time of its commission, that what they were doing was wrong, the scheme helped them to understand why they committed the offence and the implications for them of future offending.

All offenders claimed that they had decided to keep out of trouble in future. While their involvement with the scheme was often cited as a reason for this, other factors were said to have equal, or in some cases, more impact; factors such as family support, wanting to get a job, staying employed and the threat of going to court. One offender who had been to court spoke of how traumatic it was, "it was horrible, I cried all the time". What seemed to have most influenced her decision not to reoffend was seeing the photographs in court of the injuries she had caused to her victim in an assault.

Eighty-eight per cent of the offenders interviewed lived with one or both of their parents. Most offenders recognised the impact of their offending on their parents and more widely their family. Some of the offenders felt supported by their parents, to whom they could talk about the offence and the scheme.

(b) Attitudes to victims and making amends

Most offenders agreed that taking part in the scheme had helped them to recognise the effects of their offending behaviour on others, including their victims. Some offenders seemed genuinely remorseful and wanted to say sorry and make up for what they had done wrong. Most of those who had committed minor offences felt that by writing a letter or saying sorry put things right and they could move on. Others who had committed more serious offences recognised that "writing a letter was a way of letting out the shame and guilt but it can scare you when you read back the letter. I have not made up for what I did but writing the letter has made it easier to live with."

Many of the offenders felt that what happened to them was fair, while some spoke of "deserving it", of how "hard it was to write the letter" or "difficult it was to meet the victim". Others felt they had got off lightly because they did not have to go to court.

(c) Voluntariness

Most offenders responded that taking part in the process was their own choice. A few felt pressurised into taking part; this seemed more prevalent in the mediation or conferencing processes. One offender who took part in a conference did not know why, and certainly did not see his presence as optional. Another, who had also attended a conference said, "I knew I had to do whatever they asked me to". A third had no idea the mediation process was voluntary and said, "I only wrote a letter of apology to stop the people from the scheme turning up".

(d) Contact with victims

Of the 43 offenders interviewed, 15 wrote a letter of apology to the victim. In some of those cases, the offenders had chosen not to meet the victim in person because it would be too "hard", too "scary", "too embarrassing" and most of them felt that writing a letter was enough to say sorry and "put things right". A few offenders who wrote a letter of apology also wanted to meet the victim in person and were very disappointed that the victim was unwilling to meet them. They felt they could not show they were genuinely sorry unless they met. Offenders who had not been properly debriefed after their contact with the scheme still did not know, at the time of the interview, why the victim had not wanted to meet them. They were left puzzled and felt disappointed by the process.

Ten of the offenders interviewed met their victim either in a face-to-face mediation or in a restorative conference. Most of them stressed that "it was a hard thing to do", "you have to be brave to do it"; none of these felt that it was a soft option. As one offender said "it was hard, but I got a lot out of it". Some spoke of how "nerve-wracking" it was, and how "anxious" they were about meeting the victim. They also spoke of the "embarrassment" of meeting the victim and of feeling "ashamed". These responses were more prevalent among those who knew their victim.

Most of the offenders recognised the importance of saying sorry, while some of them also appreciated victims' need to have their questions answered. As one offender said "the victim has now got a face to the crime and I am a human being and not a monster".

The reaction of the victim and/or victim's family seemed a key element in whether the offender responded positively to the interaction. Where offenders were positive about meeting the victim, they spoke of the victim "being nice to them", "understanding them", or "not judging them". One offender spoke of the confidence he gained by meeting the victim and how he "had a really good feeling afterwards".

Although 80 per cent of the offenders who met their victim said that they did not know what to expect before the meeting, most recognised it was helpful to meet the victim and know how the victim felt, although the two who attended restorative conferences were less positive on this aspect.

In some cases the offender felt worse for having taken part. One said that the victim yelled at him continually; "it was a terrible experience, [the victim] kept talking about prison and trying to scare you". One offender who had taken part in a restorative conference said she felt "picked on", that the victim's mother yelled at her and that she continues to be "wound up" by the victim since the conference. The offender said that she had looked forward to the opportunity promised by the conference to resolve the conflict, but ultimately felt that it had simply subjugated her to the victim and, in doing so, had exacerbated the ongoing hostility between them.

CRIMEPICS II

During the fieldwork period, schemes were asked to use the CRIMEPICS II questionnaire with offenders engaging in restorative justice, once before the intervention and again after it. Used in this way, the instrument provides a measure of change in attitudes to offending and to victims (Frude et al., 1998).

A combination of declining activity in the schemes, slow progress of cases, and in some areas unwillingness to administer the instrument, led to only 28 offenders completing it twice: 15 of these came from Suffolk and Leicestershire (the two 'diversion' schemes) and 13 from Gloucestershire. In most cases, the second CRIMEPICS questionnaire was completed two to three months after the first. Clearly, the sample is not large enough to generate results in which strong confidence can be placed. Nevertheless, the results are worth outlining, as they point very much in one direction.

All 28 offenders completing CRIMEPICS II were juveniles (West Yorkshire declined to co-operate in the exercise). Table 4.5 shows their average (mean) scores on the four main dimensions measured by the instrument, before and after their dealings with the scheme, as well as the numbers of individuals whose scores moved up or down.

A decrease in score represents a move in the desired direction. It can be seen that the average score fell on all but one dimensions of the instrument, and that the majority of offenders showed

Table 11. Juvenile offenders' CRIMEPICS scores (Suffolk, Leicestershire and Gloucestershire combined), before and after intervention

Dimension	Mean score*		No. of scores moving:		
	Pre intervention	Post intervention	Up	Down	Unchanged
General attitude to offending	40	37	7	19	2
Victim hurt denial	7	6	3	18	7
Anticipation of reoffending	13	11	9	14	5
Evaluation of crime as worthwhile	10	10	10	7	11

* The minimum and maximum possible scores for 'general attitude to offending' are 17 and 85; for 'victim hurt denial' 3 and 15; for 'anticipation of reoffending', 6 and 30; and for 'evaluation of crime as worthwhile, 4 and 20.

improvements in attitude. The change was most consistent in the area of 'victim hurt denial', where 18 of the 28 offenders recorded lower scores, only three showing slight increases. This suggests that the offenders had as a group become considerably more aware of victims' feelings. The other scores suggest that general attitudes to offending also improved, and that most were more confident than they had been before the intervention that they would not reoffend. On the other hand, there was very little overall change in the group's views on the rather different issue of how 'worthwhile' offending is.

These findings are encouraging, but it must be reiterated that they are based on small numbers of offenders. Moreover, even if they reflect real and significant changes in attitude, whether this can be taken as evidence of the effectiveness of 'restorative justice' is open to debate. It should be noted that over half of the offenders came from the two schemes that, while placing importance on raising offenders' 'victim awareness', achieved this in the main without making contact with victims.

5.   Outcomes

Introduction

One of the key questions to be answered when assessing the impact of the schemes considered in this study is whether or not they reduced reoffending by those participating. In practice, however, the best we could do is to measure reconvictions, or in the case of young offenders, convictions and cautions. These can only be proxies for reoffending since findings from the British Crime Survey indicate that for every 100 offences committed only about three result in a criminal conviction (see, for example, Barclay, 1991).

For our adult samples we used data on reconvictions taken from the Home Office Offenders Index to identify whether or not offenders had been reconvicted of a Standard List Offence[29] within two years of sentence (for community penalties) or release (for a custodial sentence).[30]

For the samples of young offenders in two of the juvenile schemes, we used data from the Police National Computer to identify subsequent cautions or convictions within two years of the original caution.[31] In a third (Gloucestershire), the scheme had been operating for insufficient time to allow a two-year follow-up study, but as excellent local data were available – including information on the dates on which new offences had been committed – we undertook a separate one-year follow-up study based on analysis of the Gloucestershire Youth Offending Information System (YOIS). The other two juvenile schemes were both too 'young' to allow reconviction studies at this stage. We begin by looking at the reconviction data for the adult schemes before turning our attention to the juvenile offenders.

Analysis of adult offender data

West Yorkshire

Turning first to the analysis of the data from the West Yorkshire scheme, we analysed data from 270 offenders who had been referred for possible mediation during the period 1993 to 1997. Of these 170 actually participated in both direct and indirect mediation while 100 did not. These totals were reduced to 153 and 79 respectively by excluding the 38 offenders whose details could not be found in the national Offenders Index. The referrals to the scheme came either from the Police (46%) or the Probation Service (54%), with the sole exception of one from Victim Support. In the tables below, and throughout the discussion, the treatment

---

[29] Standard List offences are all indictable offences and the more serious summary offences (see Criminal Statistics for England and Wales 1999 (Cm 5001), Appendix 4A for a complete list of offences included).

[30] The offenders had all been at liberty for the two years. For further discussion of the issues surrounding the use of reconviction proxies and the choice of the (conventional) two-year follow-up period see Lloyd et al. (1994, Chapter 2). Choosing a two-year period had the advantage of allowing us to compare actual reconvictions with those predicted by the Offender Group Reconviction scheme (OGRS), discussed in more detail below, since this predictor is based on the same time period.

[31] Cases where there was no match with either the Offenders Index or the PNC were therefore excluded.

group comprised offenders with whom the scheme was able to do some mediation work. The control group in West Yorkshire was taken from those referrals where the scheme did not provide an intervention. As is apparent from Table 12, by far the most common reason for this was that the victim was unwilling to participate (89% of cases). Only in just under five per cent was the refusal of the offender to become involved with the scheme given as a reason.

For both treatment (92%) and control (93%) groups, the overwhelming number of offenders were male. The average age at which members of the treatment group were referred to the scheme was 25.4 years (the youngest was 18 and the eldest 60). For the control group the average age was slightly higher at 26.3 years (youngest 18 years, eldest 59). In terms of offenders' age at first court appearance, for the treatment group the average was 18.6 years and for the control group 19.2 years.

Table 12. Profile of offenders referred to West Yorkshire scheme

Reason	Percentage
Safety concerns	2
Offender unwilling to participate	5
Victim declined to participate	89[32]
Other	4
Total	100 (n=79)

In the treatment group, 58 per cent had received a custodial sentence for the index offence, while in the control group the figure with such a sentence was 55 per cent. In terms of previous offending behaviour, the average number of previous offences (for which convicted) for those in the treatment group was just under 12 while for the control group it was slightly higher at 14.4 (this difference was not statistically significant[33]). The inter-quartile range for the treatment group was from one to 16 offences while for the control group it was from one to 24 offences. Table 13 presents a profile of the offenders referred to the West Yorkshire scheme.

The types of index offences, that is the primary offence that led to the conviction and subsequent referral to the scheme, were, with one notable exception, broadly similar for both treatment and control groups. For example, burglary was the target offence for 31 per cent of the treatment group and 32 per cent of the control group. There did appear however to be more violent offenders in the treatment group, where for 17 per cent of offenders the target offence was one of violence, while in the control group this figure was only 11 per cent. Similarly robbery was the target offence for 14 per cent of the treatment group, and just nine per cent of the control group.

---

[32] Our interviews with the project co-ordinators suggest main reasons for refusal are concerns about safety and possible re-victimisation. This was felt to be particularly the case for female victims. Other victims were simply too traumatised to enter the mediation process. For some it is a matter of pride in not letting the offender know they are upset. More generally the co-ordinators felt that many victims were put off by their (false) perception that they be forced to confront the offender if they participated.

[33] Two tailed test, p = 0.284.

Table 13. Profile of offenders referred to West Yorkshire scheme

	Treatment Group (N=153) % males 92%	Control Group (N=79) % males 93%
Average age at referral	25.4 years	26.3 years
Average age at first court appearance	18.6 years	19.2 years
Average number of known previous offences	11.9	14.4
Percentage receiving custodial sentence for offence leading to referral	58%	55%
Average OGRS 2 score at target offence	0.58	0.58

We also had available for analysis OGRS 2 scores for all the offenders at the time they were referred to the scheme. This is a measure that predicts the probability of reconviction for an offence within two years based upon various risk factors.[34] In theory it takes values between 0 (certain not to reoffend) and 1 (certain to reoffend). For the treatment group the average OGRS 2 score was 0.58 with an inter-quartile range between 0.39 and 0.80. On the basis of this we would predict that, other things being equal (that is, without any intervention), 58 per cent of our treatment group would be reconvicted within two years (a 95% confidence interval (CI) for the proportion reconvicted is given by 0.54 to 0.62). For the control group the average OGRS 2 was also 0.58 but with a larger inter-quartile range from 0.34 to 0.83. Unsurprisingly there was no statistically significant difference between the two groups in terms of their mean OGRS 2 scores. Again on the basis of this average score we would expect 59 per cent of the control group to be reconvicted within two years (with a slightly larger 95% CI from 0.52 to 0.64).

In summary, there were few differences between the intervention group and the control group in terms of social characteristics or previous offending. Moreover, the main reason for non-intervention with the control group was the refusal of the victim to take part. The two groups, therefore, appear to be comparable for the purpose of analysis of outcomes.

Turning now to actual reconvictions in the two years after release, we see from Table 14 that whilst 44 per cent of the treatment group (total N= 153) were convicted within two years, for the control group the corresponding figure was 56 per cent. If we apply the standard two tail statistical test for the difference of two proportions (means) we find that the difference in the reconviction rates for the two groups is statistically significant at the 10 per cent level. If however our prior belief is that the intervention will reduce offending and use a one tail test the difference is significant at the five per cent level (p=0.043).

---

[34] The revised OGRS, OGRS 2, used here also includes data on history of burglary and history of breach (see Taylor, 1999, for further information of the revised OGRS and its improved predictive performance).

Table 14. West Yorkshire: percentage reconvicted of standard list offence within two years

Treatment Group	Control Group
44% (153)	56% (79)[35]

This analysis does not take into account the differences between the two groups in their a *priori* likelihood of being reconvicted. If one group were to include a greater proportion of high-risk offenders, then crude comparisons between the groups would be biased towards the other group. We can measure this risk by offenders' score on OGRS 2. In order to control for possible differences in risk of reconviction we fitted a logistic regression model[36] taking as our dependent variable reconviction within two years and using two explanatory variables: membership of treatment or control group and individual OGRS 2 score.[37] Controlling for the predicted risk of reconviction in this way leads to larger estimated differences between the two groups in favour of the treatment group.[38] In other words the crude differences in reconviction between the groups underestimates the impact the intervention would have had if the offenders in both the treatment and control had had similar OGRS 2 scores.

We explored the relationship between reconviction and risk in more detail by allocating offenders to one of four groups on the basis of their OGRS 2 score. Group 1 consists of individuals whose scores lies in the first quartile (lowest 25% in terms of risk), group 2 individuals with scores between the first quartile and the median (bottom 25 to 50%), group 3 scores between the median and the 3rd quartile (bottom 50 to 75%) and group 4 those with OGRS 2 above the 3rd quartile (75 to100%). The percentages reconvicted, the mean numbers of reconvictions and the average OGRS score within each risk category are given in Table 14. As would be expected, in both treatment and control group, the rate of reconviction and the average number of reconvictions increases with risk.

As Table 15 shows, the impact of the intervention appears much greater in the lower risk groups as compared to those in category 4 where the risk of reconviction is highest. For offenders in the lowest risk category, the treatment group had eight per cent reconvicted within two years compared with 24 per cent in the control group. This difference was also apparent when comparing mean numbers of reconvictions, where for the control group this was nearly three times that in the treatment group. In risk category 2 the difference between groups' two-year reconviction rates is slightly larger than for category 1 but the mean numbers are much closer. In risk category 3 the difference in the percentage reconvicted across the two groups

---

[35] Figures in brackets refer to total number in each group in the risk category.

[36] Logistic regression is a multivariate statistical technique used when the variable to be explained can take only one of two discrete values.

[37] We fitted models with other explanatory variables in addition to these two but were unable to find any that were statistically significant. This is not surprising given the number of variables already used in constructing OGRS 2.

[38] In addition the estimated difference is more statistically significant in the sense that the p value associated with the observed difference, under the null hypothesis that there is no difference, falls from 0.086 to 0.059.

is marginally smaller than for the lower risk categories – the gap in the mean numbers has increased. In the highest risk category 4, the difference in the percentages reconvicted is much narrower with 69 per cent of the treatment group compared to 74 per cent of the control group being reconvicted of an Index offence within the two years. However the treatment group has a mean number of reconvictions of 1.75 compared to 2.63 for the control.

Table 15. West Yorkshire: percentage reconvicted within two years, mean actual reconviction rates and mean OGRS score by OGRS risk category[39]

	Treatment Group	Control Group
Risk Category 1: Lowest 25%		
percentage reconvicted	8%	24%
mean reconviction rate	0.14	0.38
mean OGRS score	0.23	0.23
	(36)	(21)
Risk Category 2: 25%-50%		
percentage reconvicted	37%	53%
mean reconviction rate	1.05	1.18
mean OGRS score	0.49	0.49
	(41)	(17)
Risk Category 3: 50%-75%		
percentage reconvicted	64%	79%
mean reconviction rate	1.24	1.68
mean OGRS score	0.73	0.73
	(42)	(19)
Risk Category 4: Highest 25%		
percentage reconvicted	69%	74%
mean reconviction rate	1.75	2.63
mean OGRS score	0.88	0.90
	(32)	(19)

The evidence presented so far suggests that the West Yorkshire scheme produces a small, but statistically significant, reduction in reconviction rates as compared to the control group, but that the scheme is less successful with those offenders who are in the highest risk categories for reconviction as measured by OGRS 2.

However we also need to look at whether the actual reconvictions in both groups differ significantly from those predicted by OGRS 2. For the treatment group comparing the actual proportion reconvicted, 44 per cent, with that predicted by OGRS 2, 58 per cent, showed a statistically significant difference at the 0.01 significance level. There is no statistical

---

[35] Figures in brackets refer to total number in each group in the risk category.

difference, however, in the control group between the actual percentage reconvicted (57%) and the predicted percentage (58%). Hence we may conclude that the intervention in West Yorkshire is successful, not only by comparison with the control group, but also in reducing the risk of reconviction in the two year period from that predicted by OGRS 2.

As well as considering whether the intervention affects the risk of reconviction within the two-year period, it is interesting to compare the groups in terms of both the numbers of reconvictions and the number of offences leading to the reconvictions over the period. Turning first to reconvictions, among all offenders (including those with no reconvictions), we find that for the treatment group there was an average of 1.01 reconvictions per offender within two years and for the control, 1.43 – a statistically significant average difference of 0.42 reconvictions per offender.[40] Alternatively, if we consider only those offenders reconvicted at least once, we find that the average number of reconvictions was 2.28 for the treatment group and 2.54 for the control; not a statistically significant difference.

In terms of offences committed and leading to reconviction within the two-year period, the average number of offences for each member of the treatment group was 2.63 while for members of the control group the corresponding number was 3.88. Hence the intervention reduced the average number of offences by 1.25.[41] Again if we look just at those reconvicted in the period we find an average number of offences per member of the treatment group of 5.91 compared to 6.91 for control group members.[42]

A final issue to be addressed is the question of the seriousness of the offences for which offenders are reconvicted. There are clearly many different ways in which offences may be ranked in terms of their seriousness and no single approach will capture all the dimensions of the concept. The data from the OI provides information on reconviction seriousness that develops a classification proposed by a working group from the Probation Service and the Home Office in 1994. The starting point for this was to rank offences according to the maximum penalty available. This was then adjusted to take account of anomalies arising from the actual use of different penalties.[43] The result was an eight point scale ranging from A for the most serious offences to H for the least serious.

---

[40] Statistically different from zero at the 5% level using a one tail t-test.

[41] Significant at the 5% level (one tail test). In addition to control for differences in background we fitted a regression model with dependent variable number of reconvictions within two years and independent variables OGRS 2 and treatment. The treatment variable was still significant using a one tailed test (p=0.03) and the estimated average reduction in reconvictions for those in the treatment group was 0.41.

[42] This difference, however, was not statistically significant. Again we fitted a regression model to control for background using OGRS 2. The regression model suggested that being in the treatment group reduced the known number of re-offences within two years by 1.29 on average compared to the control group and that this reduction was statistically significant at the 5% level.

[43] Category A includes all 'grave offences' such as murder or manslaughter carrying a maximum penalty of life imprisonment. Robbery and assault with intent to rob are also in Category A. Category B includes other offences for which life imprisonment is a possible penalty. Category C includes domestic burglary and criminal damage. Category D includes non-domestic burglary, handling and receiving stolen goods and fraud. Theft of a motor vehicle, violent disorder, theft by an employee and various less serious fraud offences fall in category E while category F contains such offences as theft in a dwelling, theft from motor vehicles and other low level theft offences. Categories G and H are collections of low level offences against both property and the person.

Table 16. West Yorkshire: percentage reconvicted within two years by offence seriousness[44]

	Treatment Group (N=153)	Control Group (N=79)
Offence seriousness A	6%	4%
Offence seriousness B	0	0
Offence seriousness C	17%	28%
Offence seriousness D	9%	10%
Offence seriousness E	7%	16%
Offence seriousness F	23%	32%
Offence seriousness G	6%	5%
Offence seriousness H	28%	32%

Apart from categories A and G, where the actual numbers are in any case small, the treatment group has smaller percentages in each seriousness category. These differences are particularly noteworthy in category C which includes domestic burglary and criminal damage, category E which includes theft of a motor vehicle and category F which includes theft from the person and theft from motor vehicles. Overall the message from Table 16 is that the reconvictions for the treatment group are for less serious offences.

In conclusion the evidence suggests that for our sample of offenders referred to the West Yorkshire scheme, those who participated in restorative justice were less likely to be reconvicted within two years than those who did not. Members of the treatment group also have lower reconviction rates than would be expected from their OGRS 2. This is not true for those who did not receive mediation. There was also some evidence to suggest that where there were reconvictions and reoffending by those in the treatment group it was for less serious offences compared with the control group.

West Midlands

We were able to analyse reconviction and other data for 270 offenders from the West Midlands, reducing to 230 when offenders who could not be traced on the Offenders Index (OI) were excluded. Of those who were matched on the OI, 147 had participated in the scheme whilst the remaining 83 had not. For both the treatment and control groups the majority of referrals were from the Probation Service (89% and 92% respectively).

As with West Yorkshire, the treatment group consists of offenders with whom the scheme did some kind of restorative work, while again the control group comprised those where such interventions were not possible. In 28 per cent of the control group this was because the offender eventually decided not to participate, having been willing at first to do so. Other

---

[44] The base for this Table is all offenders. The number for the treatment group is 153, and 79 for the control. Percentages may sum to more than 100 since offenders may have been reconvicted of more than one offence.

reasons for not pursuing the intervention are given in Table 17. Compared to West Yorkshire these are biased towards reasons connected with the offender rather than the victim. In the West Midlands, if the victim refused to participate, the scheme usually continued to work with the offender (unlike West Yorkshire, where this would terminate the case).

Table 17. West Midlands control group: reasons for lack of intervention

Reason	Percentage
Offender unwilling to participate	28
No guilty plea	2
Contact with offender lost	2
Offender not suited to intervention	6
Resource limitations	7
Other/not known	55
Total	100 (n=83)

Table 18 presents some comparisons between the two groups. Again males dominated both groups. The average age at referral was similar in both groups and both had similar spreads of ages (the inter-quartile range being 19 to 27 years for the treatment and 19 to 28 for the control group). The treatment group had a slightly higher average age at first court appearance but this difference was not statistically significant. Both had similar inter-quartile ranges for this measure from 15 to 19 years.

Table 18. Profile of offenders referred to West Midlands scheme

	Treatment Group (N=147) % males 96%	Control Group (N=83) % males 94%
Average Age at referral	24.4 years	24.5 years
Average age at first court appearance	18.5 years	17.8 years
Average number of known previous offences	12.5	17.1
Percentage receiving custodial sentence for offence leading to referral	52%	41%
Average OGRS 2 score at target offence	0.57	0.66

Comparing the two groups in terms of their previous offending, Table 18 shows that the control group had higher average previous offending compared to the treatment group. The difference in the mean rates was statistically significant at the five per cent level. Fifty two per cent of the treatment group and 41 per cent of the control group received a custodial sentence for the offence that related to the referral.

In terms of the predicted likelihood of reconviction within two years the average OGRS 2 for the treatment group was 0.57. With 95 per cent confidence and other things being equal we would expect between 52 per cent and 61 per cent of the treatment group to be reconvicted within two years. The average OGRS 2 for the control group was 0.66 giving a 95 per cent CI prediction of between 61 per cent and 71 per cent reconvicted in the next two years. This difference in predicted reconvictions between the groups was significant at the one per cent level. For the West Midlands sample the control group differs from the treatment group in having a higher average number of previous recorded offences and a higher average risk score.

Looking now at actual rather than predicted reconvictions, Table 19 presents results calculated from the OI data on the percentage in both groups reconvicted within two years. For the treatment group the percentage who were reconvicted in the period was 44 per cent whilst the proportion of the control group reconvicted was 54 per cent. However this difference is not statistically significant at the five per cent level even if we use a one tail test, (p-value = 0.12). Hence even before controlling for risk of reconviction by using OGRS 2 we have no statistically significant difference between the two groups using conventional significance levels. It should be emphasised however that the actual difference is relatively large, that the test is only just insignificant and that this is probably due to the relatively small sample sizes.

Table 19. West Midlands: percentage reconvicted of standard list offence within two years[45]

Treatment Group	Control Group
44% (143)	54% (87)

Again, a more sensible comparison is probably between the reconviction rates after controlling for OGRS 2. Again we did this by using logistic regression with the reconviction dummy as the variable to be explained, and explanatory variables being membership of the treatment or control group and the individual's OGRS 2 score.

Unlike West Yorkshire, however, controlling for the risk of reconviction does not produce a clearer distinction between the two groups which can be attributed to the effect of the treatment. Once risk of reconviction is taken into account the difference between reconviction rates in the two groups is even less statistically significant. The lower observed rate of reconviction in the treatment group can be explained by their lower levels of a priori risk, not by participation in the programme.

---

[45] Figures in brackets refer to total number in each group in the risk category.

We explore the relationship between reconviction and risk further in Table 20, where again we have grouped offenders according to which quartile of the ranked OGRS 2 score they belong. There is no consistent picture, with the proportion reconvicted being greater in the treatment group than the control group in the lowest risk category, being 12 per cent lower in the second, two per cent less in the third category and 6.4 per cent less in the highest risk group. In terms of mean reconviction rates the control group has a lower rate than the treatment group at each risk level except the highest.

Table 20. West Midlands: percentage reconvicted within two years, mean actual reconviction rates and mean OGRS score by OGRS risk category

(Figures in brackets refer to total number in each group in the risk category)

	Treatment Group	Control Group
Risk Category 1: Lowest 25%		
percentage reconvicted	18%	14%
mean reconviction rate	0.35	0.14
mean OGRS score	0.25	0.25
	(45)	(14)
Risk Category 2: 25%-50%		
percentage reconvicted	46%	58%
mean reconviction rate	1.05	0.89
mean OGRS score	0.51	0.53
	(37)	(19)
Risk Category 3: 50%-75%		
percentage reconvicted	58%	61%
mean reconviction rate	1.22	1.07
mean OGRS score	0.73	0.75
	(42)	(28)
Risk Category 4: Highest 25%		
percentage reconvicted	62%	68%
mean reconviction rate	1.65	2.09
mean OGRS score	0.90	0.91
	(34)	(22)

As with the West Yorkshire data we next compared actual reconviction rates with those predicted by OGRS 2. For the treatment group the actual proportion reconvicted (44%) within two years is statistically significantly less than that predicted by OGRS 2 (57%).[46] Hence this suggests that the intervention has had an effect. However similar analysis of data from the control group comparing the actual percentage reconvicted (55%) with that predicted (66%) also indicates a statistically significant reduction.[47] Hence we conclude that the level of

---

[46] At the 1% significance level.
[47] This time at the 5% significance level.

reconvictions for both groups of offenders is less than predicted but this cannot be attributed to the intervention.

Turning to the numbers of reconvictions and the numbers of recorded offences within the two-year period we find no statistically significant difference between the mean number of reconvictions for the treatment (0.99) and the control (1.14), with this conclusion continuing to hold when we fitted a regression model to control for background via OGRS2. Amongst those reconvicted at least once, the mean number of reconvictions was 2.3 for the treatment group and 2.11 for the control group and again this was not statistically significant. For actual known offences committed in the two-year period the average number for the treatment group was 2.4 and for the control 2.8, again an insignificant difference both before and after controlling for background differences. For those reconvicted at least once the average number of offences was 5.5 for the treatment group and slightly less in the control group at 5.2 per offender. Again we found no evidence of any independent effect for the intervention.

Finally we compared the groups in terms of the seriousness of the known offences leading to reconvictions. These results are presented in Table 21. There does not appear to be any major difference between the two groups in the seriousness of the offences leading to the reconvictions.

Table 21. West Midlands: percentage % reconvicted within two years by offence seriousness

(percentages may sum to more than 100 since offenders may have been reconvicted of more than one offence)

	Treatment Group (N=143)	Control Group (N=87)
Offence seriousness A	3%	4%
Offence seriousness B	0	0
Offence seriousness C	9%	10%
Offence seriousness D	10%	6%
Offence seriousness E	6%	11%
Offence seriousness F	17%	32%
Offence seriousness G	9%	6%
Offence seriousness H	36%	35%

In conclusion reconviction rates for both the treatment and control groups were less than would have been expected on the basis of OGRS 2. However given that this was the case for both groups there was no evidence that being involved in mediation had any impact upon reconviction or reoffending. Further we found no evidence of differences in the numbers of reconvictions or the level of known offences between the two groups.

The adult schemes: conclusions and review

In broad terms, the retrospective analysis suggests that interventions by the West Yorkshire scheme had a significant impact on reconviction rates. A smaller proportion of the intervention group than the control group was reconvicted within two years and members of the intervention group had lower reconviction rates than was predicted by OGRS 2. On the other hand, no significant differences were found in the case of interventions by the West Midlands scheme.

We can only speculate on the reasons why the West Yorkshire scheme appeared to be successful whereas no significant impact on reconvictions was found in the West Midlands scheme. It may be, of course, that the interventions in the two schemes were markedly different in character or quality, but as we were unable to observe current cases in the West Midlands it is difficult to establish this with certainty. One clear difference, however, was that the West Yorkshire scheme worked with offenders only if the victim was willing to take part, so the level of communication between offenders and victims facilitated by scheme staff (mainly by "shuttle diplomacy") was generally higher. It is also apparent that the West Yorkshire scheme was larger in scale, more securely funded and arguably better organised, with stronger commitment from higher management. Such factors may have had an impact on staff morale and the quality of service delivery.

An alternative explanation is the fact that in West Yorkshire it was made very clear to offenders from the outset that participation in the scheme would have no bearing on their sentence, whereas in the West Midlands (where reports outlining offenders' willingness to take part were sent to the court), some may have opted to participate in the hope of being treated more leniently. Consequently they may have been less committed to the scheme's activities.[48]

Analysis of the young offender data

The analysis of reconviction data on young offenders was different in two important respects to that involving adults. First, as we used the Police National Computer (PNC), rather than the Offenders Index, data were available on cautions as well as reconvictions (the same applies to Gloucestershire, where we used a local record system, as will be discussed later). Secondly, however, OGRS is not applicable to juveniles, so we were reliant solely on comparisons with control groups, rather than being able to compare actual and predicted outcomes; this inevitably reduces the reliability of the results to some extent. We now look in turn at the data from Leicestershire, Suffolk and Gloucestershire.

Leicestershire

We collected information on 270 young offenders who had been referred to the Leicestershire Caution Plus scheme. Of these, 200 had actually participated in the scheme's activities while

---

[48] It will be remembered that about 28% of cases in the control group in the West Midlands were discontinued owing to the withdrawal of the offender post sentence. This suggests that the control group for this scheme was overall less committed to mediation than the intervention group. If, as is plausible, a lack of commitment is to some extent correlated with reoffending, one might expect the West Midlands control group, ceteris paribus, to do worse than the intervention group. The finding that it did not do worse makes even more striking the difference we found in outcomes between the West Midlands and West Yorkshire schemes.

70 had not. After attempting to match their details against information from the PNC, our total sample numbers were reduced to 145 participants and 46 non-participants. These two groups were used as the treatment and control groups, respectively. Of the 46 non-participants, five had been considered unsuitable for intervention by the scheme, nine already had other provisions in place, and the remainder declined to take part. The reasons for non-participation, of course, raise questions about the comparability of the two groups, and these will be taken into account in presenting the conclusions.

Males (83% in the treatment group, 89% in the control group) dominated both groups. The average age of referral to the scheme was broadly similar in both groups (13.7 years treatment, 14.1 years control). Sixty-seven per cent of the treatment group and 65 per cent of the control group had previous records of offending. In terms of known numbers of previous offences prior to the target offence, 19 per cent of the treatment group and 22 per cent of the control group had more than one known offence.

Table 22. Leicestershire: target offences for which offenders were referred to scheme

	Treatment Group (N=145)	Control Group (N=46)
Violence against person	12%	11%
Sexual offence	0	7%
Burglary	23%	15%
Robbery	1%	2%
Theft and fraud	24%	28%
Criminal damage	19%	13%
Drug offences	0%	4%
Other	17%	17%
Not known	2%	2%

The target offences for which the young offenders were referred are shown in Table 22. Again the two groups have broadly similar patterns with slightly larger proportions of the treatment group cautioned for burglary and criminal damage and a slightly greater percentage of the control group cautioned for theft.

Turning now to those who are cautioned or convicted within two years of the target caution date, we see from Table 23 that the control group did have a higher percentage of known recidivism. However the levels of known reconviction are very high for both groups and the difference between the two proportions is not statistically significant. On this basis we cannot conclude that the scheme had an impact on reconviction.

Table 23. Leicestershire: percentage receiving further caution or conviction within two years[49]

Treatment Group	Control Group
65%	74%
(N=145)	(N=46)

We have not allowed however for differences between the groups which, if controlled for, might lead to a different conclusion. In order to explore this possibility we fitted various logistic regression models containing different explanatory variables including age, gender, age at first offence, history of burglary and employment status. In none of the models were we able to find any evidence of statistically significant difference between the two groups.[50]

We also compared the two groups in terms of numbers and types of known offences committed within the two-year period. For the treatment group the average number was 2.1 compared to 2.8 in the control group. Again this was not statistically significant. A similar non-significant difference may be found if we look only at those young offenders who were re-cautioned or convicted at least once within the period. Again the treatment group had a smaller, *not statistically significant*, average number of offences (3.2 compared with 3.7).

In Table 24 we compare the two groups in terms of the types of offences committed within the two years. Burglary apart, the treatment group does have lower known reoffending rates for these offences. However, once again the differences are small.

Table 24. Leicestershire: percentage known to have reoffended within two years by type of offence[51]

	Treatment Group (N=145)	Control Group (N=46)
Violent offences	15%	22%
Burglary	21%	20%
Property offences	46%	52%
Criminal damage	7%	15%
Drug offences	4%	6%

Finally, it should be remembered that the control group was made up predominantly of offenders who had declined to take part in the scheme. This would suggest that its members were more likely than the intervention group to be unreceptive to attempts to change their

[49] p= 0.24 (2 tailed), p = 0.12 (one tailed).
[50] Indeed the only significant variable we were able to identify in any of the models we fitted was age. For this group the probability of known reoffending within two years increased with age. This suggests that cautioning per se (with or without additional interventions) may have some effect on younger offenders.
[51] PNC data.

attitudes towards victims – and hence that, if there were at the outset any difference between the groups in terms of risk of reconviction, it would be the control group which one would expect to produce a higher rate. This, together with the absence of significant differences on all the dimensions presented above, makes it difficult to conclude anything other than that interventions by the Leicestershire scheme had no demonstrable impact on the likelihood or patterns of reoffending within two years.

Suffolk

The results from the analysis of the Suffolk data were strikingly similar to those for Leicestershire. Levels of known reoffending were high for both the control and treatment group and there were no statistical differences between them.

We had information on 245 young offenders who were referred to the Suffolk scheme. Of these, 192 participated in the programme, while 53 did not. Matching these with PNC data left us with a final data set for analysis of 104 participants and 35 non-participants.

Of the non-participants used in the analysis the reasons for non-participation were mainly related to offender refusal or reconviction, though in four cases the offender intervention was considered unsuitable or unnecessary. As in Leicestershire, this suggests that, if anything, the control group started out with a higher risk of reconviction.

Again, males were the significant majority comprising 85 per cent of offenders in the treatment group and 82 per cent in the control. The average age at referral was 15.1 years and 15.7 years respectively. Eighty six per cent of the treatment and 89 per cent of the control had previous records of offending.

The target offences for which the offenders were referred are shown in Table 25 below.

Table 25. Suffolk: target offences for which offenders were referred to scheme

	Treatment Group (N=104)	Control Group (N=35)
Violence against person	12%	3%
Sexual offence	1%	0%
Burglary	14%	31%
Robbery	2%	3%
Theft	46%	26%
Criminal damage	7%	11%
Drug offences	2%	0%
Other	13%	17%
Not known	4%	9%

The treatment group has a smaller percentage than the control (14% compared to 31%) for the target offence of burglary, but almost twice as many, as a proportion, for theft (46% against 26%).

Table 26. Suffolk: percentage receiving further caution or conviction within two years

Treatment Group	Control Group
71%	77%
(N=104)	(N=35)

Table 26 shows the numbers cautioned or convicted within two years of the referral. As with the Leicestershire offenders the proportion known to have reoffended with the two years was high in both groups. Although the treatment group had a lower proportion of cautions and reconvictions again this difference was not statistically significant. Again we conclude that there is no evidence to support the hypothesis that the scheme had an impact.

Again we considered the possibility that controlling for differences between the two groups might allow us to detect a difference. However we were unable to find any such effect after fitting large numbers of logistic regression models to the data.[52]

The average number of known offences within the two-year period was 2.5 for each group. If we compare the average number of known offences only for those re-cautioned or convicted the average is 3.5 in the treatment group and 3.3 in the control group. Again neither of these differences are statistically significant.

Finally we present in Table 27 some data on the seriousness of offences for which offenders were re-cautioned or convicted.

Table 27. Suffolk: percentage known to have reoffended within two year by type of offence

	Treatment Group (N=104)	Control Group (N=35)
Violent offences	11%	11%
Burglary	14%	23%
Property offences	52%	54%
Criminal damage	11%	11%
Drug offences	14%	17%

---

[52] The age effect noted in the Leicestershire data was again present.

Apart from burglary the pattern of known reoffending is similar across the two groups. Yet again we find no evidence to suggest a treatment effect.

We recognise that one reason we were unable to find statistically significant effects might be due to the small numbers that were available for analysis in the control groups. For this reason we also carried out statistical analyses on the pooled data sets combining the information from both Leicestershire and Suffolk, but again could find no evidence that the interventions had any impact in reducing offending. Hence as far as we were able we have attempted to meet the argument that the absence of significant differences reported were due to the small individual sample sizes and found nothing to support it.

Gloucestershire Diversion Unit

Gloucestershire possessed an excellent computer based system (YOIS) on which details were recorded of all juvenile offenders resident in Gloucestershire who had been cautioned or charged for offences committed within the county. This was used in preference to the PNC for the outcome study in this area, as a two-year follow-up study was not possible (see below). The restriction to in-county offending is not thought to decrease the value of these data, as the great majority of juvenile offences are known to be committed close to the offender's home.[53] Otherwise, the data are more comprehensive – and probably more reliable – than those held on the PNC.

As the Gloucestershire scheme did not begin taking referrals until late 1997, insufficient time had elapsed to undertake a two-year reconviction analysis based on a significant number of cases. However, we were able to carry out analysis based on a one-year follow up of 120 cases referred to the scheme between November 1997 and December 1998, together with an equivalent analysis of a control sample of 134 young offenders making their first appearances in court during the 12 months immediately prior to the implementation of the scheme. In the great majority of cases, the latter would have been referred to the scheme had it been in operation at the time. In terms of comparability, this control group appears to be more suitable for our purposes than those available in Leicestershire and Suffolk.

However, unlike in the other two juvenile schemes, it was found that there was a significant sex difference between the intervention and control groups: 24 per cent of the former, compared with 16 per cent of the latter, were female. (Otherwise, no significant differences were found between the two groups.) The sex difference had some effect on overall known reoffending rates, and we have therefore also presented the results for males and for females separately. These are shown in Table 28.

Two initial points have to be made about these results. First, it is known that, while the great majority of young offenders referred to the scheme received some form of restorative or 'victim awareness' intervention, a few did not: we are, however, unable to identify the latter from the

[53] See, e.g., Baldwin J. and Bottoms, A.E. (1976).

YOIS data.[54] Secondly, we have based the analysis on the date on which any known *reoffending* occurred (i.e. the 'date of first new offence', which is given in every case, is preferred to the 'date of first new proceeding', as the latter can be considerably delayed: such delays are more likely to distort the results in a 12-month than a two-year follow-up analysis).[55]

Table 28. Gloucestershire Diversion Unit
Known reoffending rates (within 12 months) of juvenile offenders referred November 1997 to December 1998 and of control group making first court appearance, November 1996 to October 1997

	No. in group	No. (%) reoffending within 12 months
Males		
Intervention group)	91	40 (44%)
Control group	112	51 (46%
Females		
Intervention group)	29	8 (28%)
Control group	22	10 (46%)
All		
Intervention group)	120	48 (40%)
Control group	134	61 (46%)

It can be seen from Table 28 that a smaller proportion (40%) of the intervention group than the control group (46%) reoffended within 12 months. However, encouraging as it may be, this is not a statistically significant difference. Moreover, the difference is accounted for almost entirely by the sex differences in the compositions of the groups: females referred to the scheme reoffended considerably less than females in the control group (though this latter difference is still not statistically significant).

The young offender schemes: conclusions and review

These must inevitably be brief and to the point. A few minor differences in outcomes were found between intervention groups and control groups, in most cases indicating that those who had received scheme interventions had 'done slightly better' than their counterparts. However, none of these differences were found to be statistically significant. We pooled the Leicestershire and Suffolk samples to see if the statistical insignificance was simply a result of the small sample sizes but this had no impact on our conclusions. We were not able to pool

---

[54] scheme records indicate that 111 offenders received interventions over this period (cf. Table 1).
[55] In this case, in fact, it makes very little difference to the results whether one takes the date of new proceedings or date of new offence as the cut-off point.

the Gloucestershire data, as this was not compatible with the other two sets. On the basis of the available data, then, there is no evidence that any of the three juvenile schemes produced a significant impact on known reoffending (as measured by cautioning or reconviction rates); nor was there any strong evidence that the level of known offending might be reduced or the pattern of offences changed.

6.   Costs and cost-effectiveness of the schemes

Introduction

To evaluate cost-effectiveness, information is needed about both costs and outcomes. Ideally we would use information about prevented offences as an indicator of outcome. In practice we can only measure offences that result in reconvictions, an underestimate of actual offending. The impact of the schemes on reconvictions has been described in Chapter 5. This section describes the approach to estimating the costs of the schemes and links these to the measured outcomes in order to evaluate cost-effectiveness. For the adult schemes, an outcome in the form of an effect on reconvictions was found. As no alternative interventions would have taken place in the absence of the adult schemes, the evaluation focuses on the costs of achieving the outcomes. No effective outcome was identified for the juvenile schemes, so costs were compared with the costs of alternative disposals.

In order to estimate the comprehensive costs of the interventions it is necessary to understand the process, identify the level of resources used, attach a value to those resources and link the value to appropriate measures of output and outcome (Allen and Beecham, 1993). The processes have been described in Chapter 3. The principal resource used in the schemes was staff time, so it was important to establish a value, or unit cost, for this input. We start by describing the process used to identify the unit costs of staff time and other inputs for each of the schemes. Some parts of the process were "fixed" in that they did not vary across cases, so the unit costs for each of these were also identified. However, where possible we have identified the individual level of resources attributable to each case in order to explore how costs vary with the characteristics of cases. We describe how we identified the level of staff input associated with individual cases and how variations in costs were associated with characteristics of cases and the nature of the interventions. We draw together information about levels of resources and unit costs to estimate the costs per case. Finally, we link evidence about effectiveness in order to assess the cost-effectiveness of the schemes. Appendix C provides further details about the cost estimation for each scheme.

Estimation of unit costs

A bottom-up approach was adopted when estimating the costs of the two adult and five juvenile schemes. This allowed an accurate analysis to be made of the costs of time spent by staff on specific case activities. It was also possible to estimate the costs of time-consuming activities that might be under-represented or missed from scheme expenditure accounts (training volunteers, for example, or management input). In most of the schemes, non-restorative justice activities were undertaken by the same staff members, or on the same premises as restorative justice work, so a top-down approach to dividing expenditure would have risked allocating inappropriate costs to the specific activities in which we were interested.

A unit cost was constructed for the time of every service professional involved in the intervention at each of the schemes. The major elements of the unit cost are salary and payroll on-costs, but other direct revenue items (such as heating and lighting) have been included for all schemes, plus an estimate of the opportunity cost of capital (office space and equipment). It was also important to include arrangements within the individual scheme for training, supervision and the provision of administrative support.

Where volunteers were involved in the mediation process, there would be no (or little) direct cost to the scheme itself, but activity information was collected which allowed an estimation of the cost of the input should employed staff be used. In all schemes where the volunteers were undertaking work that might be undertaken by paid staff in different settings, volunteer time was costed at the equivalent staff rate as volunteers may not be available in other settings. The costs of staff time spent recruiting, training, supervising and supporting volunteers were also included.

Each scheme operated differently and presented its own challenges to cost calculation, so the approach was adapted to each set of circumstances. Naturally, the bottom-up approach has its drawbacks. Activities that are not case-specific may be under-estimated (time spent on general administrative tasks, for example). Time diary information can assist in this process, but was not seen as a feasible option in this evaluation. In linking the resources used to activities undertaken, every effort has been made to ensure that the cost of cases that needed to be processed but were not accepted by the schemes was allocated to the costs of the cases where work was undertaken.

It is also difficult to take into consideration the full cost implications of setting up a new service. However, the evolving AMENDS scheme in Waltham Forest was able to supply data detailed enough to allow costs to be calculated both top-down and bottom-up for the first two years of its existence. It was possible, therefore, to assess the investment necessary to set up and sustain the scheme as it developed. Some information was also available about the set-up costs incurred by the scheme in Mansfield.

The first stage of the costing process was to estimate unit costs in a way that could be linked directly to the way resources were measured. The key component in the schemes was staff time. For the most part, therefore, direct and indirect costs were linked to levels of staff activity. Expenditure and salary data were taken from the period during which the retrospective cases were drawn and uprated to 1998/99 price levels. Below, we outline the unit costs relevant to each of the schemes and describe the set-up costs where these were available. Data relating to staff pay and working conditions, overheads and capital costs was requested from each of the schemes, and were discussed by a researcher at interview with a senior member of staff at the scheme. Where reliable, recent, accounts information was available; this was used as a basis for the calculation of the unit cost of each staff member's time. In most cases, it was possible to aggregate such unit costs from scheme-specific information. However, the same level of detail was not available for all schemes so, in some cases, minor compromises had to be made. The end product of this exercise was a table for each scheme identifying the comprehensive cost of employing each member of staff involved in restorative justice activities, and indicating the source of all data used in its compilation (Hallam and Netten, 2001). Due to concerns about confidentiality, these tables are not reproduced in this report. In the section below, the main sources of data for each of the schemes are indicated.

West Yorkshire Victim Offender Units

For West Yorkshire, five elements of the cost of the intervention were identified:

- the cost of co-ordinator time on the case
- the cost of the referral process and other activities
- the cost of mediator time (paid on a sessional basis)
- the cost of travel and subsistence expenses
- volunteer expenses.

To calculate the unit cost of a co-ordinator's time in each of the four local divisions (Leeds, Bradford, Wakefield/Kirklees and Calderdale), salary and payroll on-costs were taken from division-specific revenue accounts information. Divisional running costs came from the same source, and asset rental and head office costs (including a central training budget) were apportioned according to the advice of a senior finance executive. Staff worked 37 hours per week and were estimated to work 44 weeks per annum (assuming five weeks' annual leave and five days' sick leave). Co-ordinator hourly costs ranged between £23 and £32 per hour.

Sessional mediators were paid on the same basis throughout the scheme and cost £9.30 per hour at 1998/99 prices. In order to estimate the costs of unmeasured activity, the referral process and other activities were estimated to take up ten per cent of total process activities. The cost of these then was allocated to those cases where active restorative justice work took place (£142 per case).

'Volunteers' in this scheme were trainee sessional workers who shadowed paid workers but did not undertake any independent activities that would have to be paid for in another scheme. They received expenses, but no other direct payments, although the cost of training volunteers is an important element in the overall costs of the scheme. If it were assumed that volunteers were paid during the training process, the cost per case would be of the order of £1 to £2 greater.

West Midlands Probation Service Victim Offender Unit

It was particularly problematic estimating costs for the West Midlands scheme, as there were no reliable accounts and activity data. Information was collected about known salary and on-costs, office space and equipment during 1995-96, the main year from which retrospective cases were taken. Details were then uprated to 1998-99 price levels. Unit costs were calculated for the unit manager, a mediator and an administrative assistant, all of whom had different annual leave entitlements, but worked 37 hours per week. Five days' sick leave was added and an hourly unit cost calculated by dividing the total cost by the number of working hours in the year. Total costs included estimated direct and indirect overheads. The unit manager estimated that she spent 20 hours per week on supervision and general mediation activities: the remainder of her time was taken up by non-restorative justice activities. The administrative assistant worked only half time on mediation paperwork. The cost of the time spent by these staff members on relevant tasks was loaded onto the unit cost of the two mediators: once supervision and administration costs were included, West Midland mediator costs were estimated as £23 per hour.

AMENDS

It was identified above that the AMENDS scheme was relatively new at the time of the study so it was possible to investigate the costs of setting up the scheme. Cost information is taken from details of actual salary and payroll on-costs, revenue costs (including office overheads) as published in the chairman's report for 1998-99 and apportioned costs, as estimated by the manager, for 1999-2000. Major expenditure on fittings and equipment was annuitised over five years at a discount rate of six per cent. Premises costs were linked to individual members of staff and were based on the annuitised expected new build costs of office space for social workers (Netten et al., 1999).

The direct costs of setting up the scheme were £63,108 in all, or £31,554 per annum, over the first two years. Much of the cost was absorbed by immediate activities once the scheme was taking referrals (casework, work with volunteers) but time spent on multi-agency networking represents a longer-term investment in the scheme. It would be appropriate to spread the cost of networking at the start of the scheme's life, perhaps over a period of five years. This gives a cost per annum of £2,150 for networking and reduces the overall set-up cost to £24,640 per annum. Fundraising activities comprised a vital and time-consuming element of the co-ordinator's work over this period. Approximately £18,000 was invested (over two years) in the co-ordinator's work to raise funds.

In addition to the costs of activities estimated above, there were cost elements associated with the training courses for volunteers during this period. These included the external trainer's fee and expenses associated with running the courses. These items add an additional £5,150 to the cost over two years (£2,570 per annum).

Allowing for annuitisation (as described above) and for volunteer expenses, the total invested over this period was £54,800. Of this, 33 per cent was invested in fundraising, 32 per cent on case work, 18 per cent on the recruitment and support of volunteers, nine per cent on training volunteers and eight per cent on networking activities.

Between April 1998 and the end of 1999, AMENDS received 259 referrals, 38 of which resulted in some kind of active intervention (see Appendix B). A crude calculation of the number of cases worked on per month allows us to estimate 32 in total during the 'first' period (up to September 1999). The total (annuitised) investment in the scheme resulted in 32 cases at a cost of £1,710 per case.

The fieldwork was undertaken during the second phase of the scheme. During this period the scheme had a full-time manager, a full-time co-ordinator and a full-time administrator. Unit costs were calculated for each of these professionals although, because the manager's direct involvement with this particular project was reduced considerably from January 2000, it was decided to use her unit cost as a basis for calculating an additional 'fixed cost' per case (see below). As in the initial period, volunteers undertook much of the casework.

The costs of sample cases were estimated on the basis of time spent directly by the administrator (£16 per hour), the co-ordinator (£22 per hour), volunteers (costed on the basis of paid sessional workers in West Yorkshire), the police and other agencies. However, it is also important to include the use of resources that were not measured as direct input to cases.

These 'fixed costs'[56] included input by the scheme manager, the co-ordinator's time spent on general management and administration, administrator time not associated with specific cases, training and recruitment costs of volunteers (£149 per volunteer) and an allowance to reflect the input of the YOT officer to the referral process. The direct costs of cases where no contact was made were allocated to those cases where contact was made, on the basis that 55 per cent of the cases assessed did get some level of activity. (This estimate was based on information supplied by the scheme). Such costs added a further £10 to the cost of active cases. In total, these elements added £330 per active case on the basis of an assumption of 96 active cases per year. This reflected the level of activity in the first few months of 2000 when the fieldwork took place. The scheme reported that there was capacity for 240 cases per year: this would reduce fixed costs per case to £160.

Gloucestershire Diversion Unit

One manager and three practitioners staffed the Diversion Unit at Gloucester at the time of the research. The three diversion officers had different agency backgrounds and were seconded on a one-year basis (with the option of a second year). One was an education welfare officer, one a police officer and one a social worker. As the work was carried out on a generic basis, an average unit cost was estimated for diversion officer time (£22 per hour). Mean salary and payroll on-cost information was taken for the three professionals. This was supplemented with facility accounts information relating to travel, training, office overheads and an estimate to cover management overheads based on input discussed at interview. Premises costs were estimated on the same basis as AMENDS. The unit manager's unit cost was calculated in the same way (although this was used as a basis for calculating a 'fixed cost' add-on per case,

---

[56] Throughout the term fixed costs has been used for those costs that were necessary to have been incurred for the cases to be processed but have not been linked to individual variations in input levels to those cases.

due to his involvement in other activities: see below). Administrative support was provided to the Unit on an ad hoc basis, but the manager estimated that the Unit's work occupied a clerical worker for 2.5 days per week, so a suitable amount was added to the unit costs of the manager and diversion officer. The manager worked 37 hours per week and the diversion officers 38 hours per week. Forty-four working weeks were assumed per annum, allowing for holiday entitlement and sick leave.

Although the manager did undertake some casework the majority of his input was through general management responsibilities for the Unit. This was estimated to cost £80 per case. Other 'fixed' costs included the initial assessment and subsequent review by the Young Offenders' Review Group (YORG) and by the team as a whole (£70 per case). In 20 per cent of cases there were action plans drawn up, but for a variety of reasons they did not proceed. Loading the costs of these cases on to those where there was an intervention adds a further £44 per case.

Volunteers were not involved in the cases at the time of the fieldwork. Should the training of volunteers be included, this would add £60 per case. However, given the lack of active input by volunteers, this amount has been excluded from the estimates described above.

Gloucester also undertakes family group conferencing. No examples of this were included in our sample but the costs were estimated for those conferences that took place in 1998 (seven) and 1999 (six). Training costs were included in the 1998 costs (£710 per conference), but not in 1999 conferences (£560 per conference). Appendix C shows the breakdown of these costs in more detail.

Leicestershire Young Offenders Diversion Scheme

At the time the research was carried out, there were four people employed at the Leicester scheme: a scheme manager, an interventions manager, an administrative assistant and a clerical assistant. All staff were working full time and exclusively for the scheme. Salary and on-cost details, office overheads and travel expenses were obtained from facility accounts. Capital costs were estimated on a market valuation of the type of building and management overheads calculated from input details obtained at interview. All staff worked 37 hours per week, with 27, 28 or 29 days' holiday per annum. An allowance of five days' sick leave was added to this entitlement. Unit costs were as follows: scheme manager (£22 per hour), interventions manager (£18 per hour) and administrator (£13 per hour). The actual intervention was undertaken by volunteers who, as in other schemes, were costed using the rates paid to sessional workers in West Yorkshire for the purposes of comparison with other schemes. Additional costs that were allocated to each case included the costs of a panel meeting (£144 per case referred to the scheme), an action meeting (£22), costs of training and supporting volunteers (£150 per case). The action meeting included the administration of the panel caution.

The costs of unsuitable cases being assessed were incorporated in the process of estimating the cost of panel meetings. The cost of action meetings also includes an estimate of time spent by professionals attending meetings that were cancelled because offenders failed to attend. If sex offenders were referred to the panel additional assessment costs were estimated as £520 per case. No such cases were included in our sample.

Mansfield Restorative Conferencing Programme

The vast majority of start-up funding for the Mansfield scheme was spent on training activities. This included direct training for two sergeants and 12 constables. In all £5,000 was spent on various courses and items such as printed material. Further expenditure and time has been spent on training to extend the activities beyond the immediate scheme.

The police ran the scheme. Unit costs were calculated for three ranks of police officers. Nottingham Constabulary supplied information about terms and conditions of work, pay scales and payroll on-costs, and items such as uniform allowance. Costs were calculated on the basis of a 40-hour week and between 25 and 28 days' annual leave, plus the estimate of five days' sick leave. Unit costs were as follows: Inspector (£34 per hour), a sergeant (£27 per hour) and a constable (£22 per hour).

Neither retrospective nor prospective information was available for Mansfield so case cost information could only be based on estimated levels of activity. Appendix C identifies some estimated costs. However, these should be treated with considerable caution as independent verification of estimated levels of inputs to cases frequently found that these were much higher (see below). Moreover, allocation of costs of activities not directly associated with cases was particularly difficult to establish for this scheme.

Suffolk County Council (Youth Justice) Caution Plus Scheme

The Suffolk Caution Plus scheme functions in three separate districts. For the purposes of cost calculation, the process is similar in each of the three, so costs were based on data collected from one team. Members of the social work team, none of whom were exclusively employed for this purpose, carried out the caution plus work. Specific salary details for 1998-99 were obtained from the scheme, and payroll on-costs and office overheads were obtained from facility accounts. Scheme workers estimated travel costs and an element was added to cover capital and management overheads. Unit costs were estimated for the team manager (£22 per hour, on the basis of 37 working hours per week and 44 working weeks per annum) and the co-ordinator (£15 per hour, 37 hours per week, 45 weeks per annum). Sessional workers were paid expenses of £6 per hour. Again, for the purposes of comparison with other schemes, sessional worker costs were also estimated on the basis of payments made in West Yorkshire (£9.30 per hour). Other costs included:

- the costs of assessment by a panel
- the costs of administering the caution
- the costs of a home visit to assess the case
- the costs of training sessional workers
- the costs of management and administrative support.

The costs of the home visit were adjusted to reflect an assumption of 10 to 15 per cent of cases that were assessed as unsuitable for any further work. In total these fixed costs came to £100. Fixed costs were generally lower for this scheme compared with other schemes as it was run alongside other activities, so that cases only incurred marginal costs of general support. For example, the panel meeting would have been held in the absence of the scheme so the cost per case only reflected cases that were referred to 'caution plus'.

Resources used by the schemes

Two approaches were used to identify the level of variable inputs to cases. First, researchers identified any information available on retrospective files that gave an indication of level of input. Second, data were collected for a prospective sample of cases. Recorded levels of input were used both to predict the costs for cases where no information was available and to adjust estimated levels of input.

West Yorkshire victim offender units

In West Yorkshire information about time spent by co-ordinators and sessional workers was included in retrospective files. However, the information was not routinely recorded in all cases. Among the 167 cases that actively participated in mediation, information about co-ordinator input was available for 41 cases and about sessional mediator input for 36 cases. Further resource use information was collected about nine cases that were underway and completed at the time of the study. The majority of cases for which any resource data were available were in Wakefield. No information about resource use for actively mediated cases was available from Bradford.

Information about retrospective and prospective cases was combined to investigate causes of variation in co-ordinator and sessional mediator time. The objective was to predict input for those cases where there was no information about resource use. It should be borne in mind that little consistency of practice was found across West Yorkshire and that current practice may differ somewhat from practice in the past. This, together with the small numbers of cases meant that estimated levels of resource use should be treated with some caution.

Input by sessional mediators was 8.3 hours per case on average. In the majority of cases the number of hours spent was within a relatively narrow band (inter-quartile range = 4.5 hours) but two cases had in excess of 30 hours each spent on them. Both of these cases involved face-to-face mediation between victim and offender in prison. A considerable amount of time would have been spent travelling. As would be expected from the role that was played by co-ordinators (including training sessional workers, supervision and meetings), their direct input was rather less, 1.9 hours on average (SD=1.8 hours).

Expected causes of variation in the time spent on cases included characteristics of offenders (such as age, gender and offence), victims (such as number and type) and information about process (such as method of approaching victims and whether there was any face to face contact between victim and offender). None of these factors was found to be associated with variation in the number of sessional mediator hours.

Two factors were found to be significantly associated with co-ordinator hours. More time was spent on the case if:

(a) the offender was unemployed

(b) the contact with the victim (after the initial approach) was made by letter.

The contact method probably reflects the process of chasing the victim for a response to the initial contact. Information was only available for 12 cases where input data were not available so only employment status was used to predict co-ordinator input. In practice, the proportion unemployed was very similar among the cases for which co-ordinator input information was and was not available (73 and 76% respectively).

In order to estimate comprehensive costs we should incorporate the costs borne by other agencies. In neither of the adult schemes were other agencies routinely involved with cases. One objective of the prospective sample was to identify if there were inputs from other agencies. Of the nine cases, one had a ten-minute discussion with a probation officer. However, another case involved spending over seven hours with a probation officer. This suggested that although there would be occasional knock-on effects for other agencies, these would rarely be substantial. It was not possible to include an estimate of these on the basis of the data collected.

West Midlands Probation Service Victim Offender Unit

For West Midlands no direct data were available about resources used for individual cases. The unit manager estimated that each case took between 12 and 15 hours, slightly higher than the number of hours spent on cases in West Yorkshire (10.2). In all, 132 cases were dealt with during 1995-96. The total number of mediator hours available during the period corresponds with the estimated level of input per case. However, there is some concern that this estimate does not allow for the costs of those cases where the intervention was minimal. In such instances the estimated cost of the activity should be loaded onto those cases where an activity did take place. Case files over a number of years indicated that about a third of all cases had 'no action' of any kind, and a further five per cent involved some action, such as a telephone call, or letter written to court, but no work with the offender.

AMENDS

Only prospective case material was available for AMENDS. Information was available in about 25 cases, covering 34 offenders. Of the 25 cases, 17 were active in that the offender or the offender's family was contacted directly and some activity appeared to have taken place. The others appeared to only include administrative activity with some liaison with YOT officers and/or the police. For these cases the average level of input was 6.5 hours in total. In three instances the cases were not yet closed. These were included in the analysis as they had all been started towards the start of the sampling period (and had been open around five months), so excluding them would have biased the sample towards the shorter cases. This should be borne in mind when interpreting the information about costs of cases. Higher levels of input were associated with the three cases where there was contact with victims: an average of 14.7 hours per case.

Gloucestershire Diversion Unit

Information was available retrospectively about numbers of meetings, telephone calls and letters rather than time spent. Prospective information was available for 23 cases, two of which did not proceed to an intervention. Prospective data included information about number of visits, meetings, telephone calls and letters and detailed time breakdown. In only one case was the scheme manager directly involved, for the most part diversion officers did all of the scheme's work. In total scheme staff spent an average of 9.7 hours per case.

There was much more involvement by other professionals than in other schemes. Social workers, probation officers and/or police officers were involved in seven cases (33 per cent). These other professionals added just over an hour's input to the 21 sample cases, costing on average £28 per case.

The small numbers meant that no significant association was found with characteristics of the case or process information for the prospective cases. Contact had been made with victims in five cases, two of which resulted in further contact. Although in other schemes there was evidence of higher levels of input where there had been contact with victims, this was not the case in Gloucester, where time input by the scheme staff and total costs (including non scheme staff) were in fact slightly lower.

However, the number of visits was a good predictor of input level, explaining 50 per cent of the variation in Diversion Officer time. Information about expected "fixed" costs per case, average levels of inputs by other professionals, average levels of direct input by the manager, and number of visits by Diversion Officers were used to predict the costs of the retrospective cases (see Appendix C).

Leicestershire Young Offenders Diversion Scheme

Estimates of the amount of time spent on cases were available for 110 retrospective cases and inputs to prospective cases were identified for 13 cases. Adjustments were made to the prospective data to avoid double counting the costs of the assessment process. Nevertheless, the time recorded on prospective cases was much higher than estimated time spent by managers and volunteers on retrospective cases (multiples of 3 and 2 respectively). In the prospective sample the average number of hours spent by managers per case was just under three hours. Volunteers spent 9.6 hours, giving 12.5 hours in total. This compared with a total estimate of less than six hours retrospectively. There had been no major changes in the schemes; the difference was due to the limited information on which retrospective estimates were based. As a result the retrospective data were adjusted when estimating costs to reflect the higher levels of inputs found on the prospective cases.

However, retrospective data did reflect variation in levels of inputs allowing an analysis of what factors affected the amount of time spent on cases. Volunteer input was only associated with indicators of type of activity (such as preliminary interview only). However, the level of management hours was associated with gender and type of offence. Specifically, female juveniles were associated with a lower level of input unless they had committed a violent offence (assault or ABH). In these instances the level of input was significantly higher (p<.05). This may be due to the nature of the offender resulting in additional caution by the manager when assessing the case and allocating it to a volunteer. This scheme was unusual in that there were ten cases where the offender was female and the offence involved violence. In most other schemes only one or two cases fell into this category.

Inputs from other professionals were all at the early assessment stages. No other involvement was recorded.

Mansfield Restorative Conferencing Programme

No information was available for Mansfield other than time spent on example cases (see Appendix C). These estimates were regarded as underestimates of actual time spent.

Suffolk County Council (Youth Justice) Caution Plus Scheme

As in Leicestershire estimates were made about levels of inputs from the material available in the retrospective files based on the researchers' knowledge of how the scheme operated in practice. Estimates were provided for all 133 cases. Information was also collected about nine prospective cases in one of the districts. Again the level of inputs was much higher (twice) than the estimated input from retrospective files. In this district the co-ordinator undertook all the work, as there were no volunteers. Consultation with the respondent and the researcher suggested that the retrospective estimates were likely to be underestimates of the level of input to cases. Once adjusted on the basis of the prospective cases the average total level of input was eight hours per case.

The unadjusted levels of input were investigated to see if they were related to case characteristics. Higher levels of input were associated with being a female offender ($p<.05$), being female and having a violent offence ($p<.05$) and the case involving multiple victims ($p<.1$). Only three of the 133 cases fell into the category of being female and violent. In only one case was there any direct contact with the victim. This case did have a higher than average level of staff input ($p<.05$).

There was some involvement by other professionals, but this was very limited: for example, a psychologist in one case.

Cost per case

Combining information about levels of inputs and unit costs allows us to estimate the cost per case. Because of limited information about individual cases, these were based on expected costs given the characteristics of the intervention and the case (see Appendix C for details). Table 29 shows the estimated cost per case for all the schemes where information about individual levels of inputs was available. For those schemes that used volunteers, estimates are shown both including a valuation for volunteer time based on the cost of employing sessional workers used in West Yorkshire, and excluding this cost.

Adult schemes

The predicted average cost per case for the intervention group in West Yorkshire was £296, lower than the average cost for the 39 cases where full information was available: £347 (95 per cent confidence interval: £318 to £375). This difference reflects the very uneven distribution of cases for which full information was available from the different divisions within West Yorkshire.

Information about the costs of West Midland's cases are not provided in Table 29 as lack of information about individual cases meant it was not possible to identify the mean or median cost per case. The unit cost and input estimates for West Midlands result in the estimated cost of a case lying between £280 and £350, with a mid-point of £315 at 1998-99 price levels. If we adjust the estimated number of hours per case to allow for minimal input to 35 per cent of cases, the average cost for those cases where significant activities took place would rise to £500.

The evidence suggests that, despite the different approach to administering the schemes, the two adult schemes cost a similar amount per case. Uncertainty about the assumptions made in the cost estimation process means that these estimates need to be treated with some caution. Nevertheless, they provide us with a basis for considering their relative cost-effectiveness.

Juvenile schemes

With the exception of Suffolk, the costs of the juvenile schemes were rather higher than the costs of the adult schemes.[57] The costs of exemplar cases for the Mansfield scheme were also lower (between £144 and £254, see Appendix C), but these estimates need to be treated with considerable caution. The direct evidence about resources used by schemes tended to suggest that initial estimates underestimated the level of inputs required. When making comparisons it is also important to remember that the costs of the Gloucester scheme included nearly £30 attributable to external professionals.

The Suffolk Caution Plus scheme was run very much as an adjunct to other Youth Offending Team activities so did not need to set up specific processes for referral and assessment. Such processes mean that the cost of such activities all have to be loaded onto those cases that do result in specific interventions. The costs of all the self contained schemes, but particularly AMENDS, were very dependent on the expected level of activity overall. If full capacity for AMENDS (estimated at 240 cases per year) were reached the average cost would drop to £257 per case. However, should the number of cases where action takes place fall to 50 cases per year, the cost would rise to £675 per case.

Table 29. Predicted costs per case

| Scheme | Number of cases | Cost per case | | | |
		Mean	Median	Max	Min
Adults					
West Yorkshire	177	296	276	651	199
Juveniles[58]					
AMENDS	17	422 (354)	416 (360)	556 (416)	361 (328)
Gloucester	156	451	411	1101	273
Leicestershire	200	408 (334)	407 (334)	594 (381)	331 (319)
Suffolk	133	244 (226)	264 (240)	350 (300)	120 (1240)

When using estimates that include a valuation for the cost of volunteer time some care should be used. The cost of recruitment, support and high level of turnover of volunteers may not be reflected in input to paid sessional workers or permanent staff. Moreover, the way volunteers use their time might be different from paid workers.

Factors associated with variations in time spent on the cases were discussed above. More time was spent on cases where there were female violent offenders and cases with multiple victims.

---

[57] Although it should be borne in mind that it was not possible to estimate the knock on costs to other agencies for adult schemes and the information about these costs for juvenile schemes was also limited.

[58] Bracketed figures show the costs excluding the cost of volunteer time.

These are the factors that would be expected to be associated with higher costs. In Gloucester, although the one case that involved a violent female offender was not associated with higher scheme staff inputs, the total costs were higher because of the involvement of non-scheme professional staff. For the most part however, the high proportion of costs that were invariant across cases meant the levels of statistical significance of the relationship between case characteristics and costs were somewhat lower. It was interesting to note that female offenders who had not committed a violent offence were associated with lower costs in Leicestershire and higher costs in Suffolk. This is probably attributable to attitudes within the schemes to types of offender rather than any intrinsic attribute of female offenders.

Cost-effectiveness

The evaluation of the effectiveness of the schemes was described in Chapter 5. As no effect was found for juvenile schemes, the only comparison to be made is with the cost of the alternative.

Adult schemes

For the adult schemes, indicators of outcome include preventing one offender reoffending during the following two years, number of prevented offences and number of prevented convictions. As identified above, the data were based on reconvictions, and as such were an underestimate of actual reoffending. Table 30 draws together the outcome results reported in Chapter 5 with the estimated cost of processing cases in the adult schemes in order to identify the cost of achieving these outcomes. As the schemes were both in addition to other sentences or interventions no costs were attributed to the alternative. For the purposes of the table, the mid-point estimate of £315 per case was used for West Midlands. For West Yorkshire we used the average predicted cost for all cases in the intervention group for whom outcome data were available: £300 per case.

In all cases the outcomes represent events over the subsequent two years. Table 30 illustrates three ways of representing the outcome of the intervention: number of prevented offences (based on the number of offences for which people were convicted), number of prevented convictions, and preventing any reoffending at all (represented by the probability of having any conviction during the period). This last could be seen as the ultimate objective: turning people from criminal activity altogether. The outcome is the difference between the experimental and control group on predicted probability. So, for example, in Chapter 5 it was reported that the average number of offences committed by the experimental group in West Yorkshire was 2.63 and among the control group 3.88 per case. The difference (1.25) is the outcome that we attribute to the scheme. In order to identify the cost of achieving this outcome we divide the cost per case (£300) by the number of prevented offences per case: £240 per prevented offence.

An alternative to making comparisons with the control group is to compare the probability of reconviction within two years, based on the characteristics of the cases using OGRS 2, with the actual level of reconviction. In Chapter 5 we reported that the predicted chance of being reconvicted among the experimental group in West Yorkshire was 0.58, compared with 0.44 who were actually convicted. The reduction in probability is thus 0.14: a larger reduction than when the comparison is made with the control group. This is because the experimental group included a higher proportion of high-risk offenders than the control group. As a consequence the estimated cost per case of diverting people from being convicted at all during the two years is lower (£2,140 compared with £2,520 when the effect on reconviction is based on the control group).

A third option is to make use of the OGRS 2 risk categories identified in Chapter 5. We classify cases in both the experimental and control groups in terms of their risk of reconviction and then compare them on each measure of outcome. The difference in probability of being reconvicted and number of offences committed was not found to be statistically significant within the groups (see Table 14). However, given that the relationship is significant overall, this is probably due to the smaller sample size of the groups. The reduction in effect of deterring individuals in the highest risk category has the effect of trebling the cost per offender prevented from reoffending. However, because these offenders tend to commit more offences, the cost per prevented offence drops by 70 per cent compared to the next highest risk category.

The cost per prevented conviction is of interest as we can compare this to the cost to the criminal justice system of a conviction. The average cost per person proceeded against in the courts (including the cost of the subsequent sentence) is £2,780 at 1998-99 prices (Harries, 1999), much higher than the overall £710 per prevented conviction found for West Yorkshire. However, the savings to the criminal justice system may be very limited for the two lowest risk groups. For these groups the cost per prevented reconviction was £1,300 and £2,300. Lower risk groups may be more likely to be heard in the magistrates' courts where the average cost of a proceeding and subsequent sentence was £820 at 1998-99 prices (Harries, 1999). The cost per prevented conviction for the highest risk cases (£340) compares very favourably with the cost of Crown Court proceedings and sentence (£33,500 at 1998-99 prices, Harries, 1999).

Sensitivity analysis investigates the impact of different assumptions on costs and on the conclusions drawn. As discussed above, allowing for varying characteristics of cases had very little impact on estimated cost per case. Using the 95 per cent confidence interval estimates of average costs the conclusions drawn above would not be any different, whether observed or predicted costs were used. An alternative approach to identifying how sensitive the conclusions are to the estimated cost is to use the national average cost of a conviction as a basis for comparison. The question then is, given the level of effectiveness demonstrated by the scheme, how costly would the intervention have to be in order for us to revise our judgement about cost-effectiveness. On this basis, in order for the West Yorkshire intervention to be cost neutral to the criminal justice system the cost of a case would need to be nearly four times the current estimated cost: £1,170.

Table 30. Cost of outcomes of adult schemes

Comparison with control group	Prevented offences within two years		Prevented reconvictions within two years		Prevented any Reconviction within two years	
	Number per offender	Cost per prevented offence (£)	Number per offender	Cost per prevented conviction (£)	Reduction in probability	Cost per offender stopped from reoffending (£)
West Yorkshire Experimental compared with control	1.25	240	0.42	710	0.12	2,520
Controlling for OGRS 2 score					0.14	2,140
Comparing with control group using OGRS 2[59] risk groups:						
Low risk (cat 1)	0.61	490	0.24	1,250	0.16	1,940
Medium risk (cat 2)	0.93	320	0.13	2,310	0.16	1,840
Moderate risk (cat	0.87	350	0.44	680	0.15	2,060
High risk (cat 4)	2.85	110	0.88	340	0.05	6,120
West Midlands Experimental compared with control	0.44	720	0.15	2,100	0.12	2,940
Controlling for OGRS 2 score					0	N/A

In Chapter 5 it was reported that West Midlands was not found to have a statistically significant impact on reconviction or reducing the number of offences brought before the courts. Nevertheless, Table 30 includes the cost of preventing reconvictions and offences in the West Midlands scheme, because the lack of statistical significance could be due to sample

---

[59] See Chapter 5 for definition of risk categories.

size. However, once adjusted for the predicted level of reoffending through OGRS 2, there is no significant effect so no more detailed estimate of costs for cases in different risk categories is shown.

Juvenile schemes

In some instances the juvenile schemes were described as diversion schemes, which suggests that the alternative would have been prosecution. The average cost of a magistrates' court proceedings (excluding sentence) was £550 (Harries, 1999) so, should the average cost have been incurred all of the schemes would be less costly. However, the types of case that might have been diverted were likely to be lower cost, if only because they would have pleaded guilty. The average cost of cases where there was a guilty plea was £486 in magistrates' courts (Home Office personal communication 2001). Moreover, for the most part, the schemes' activities were provided as an alternative to a caution. The cost of a caution was estimated as £20 (based on being administered by a sergeant at the mid-point of the scale). This suggests that for all the schemes the costs of the interventions exceeded the cost of the alternative. For most of the schemes no effect was found, in the others it was not possible to identify outcomes. This does not preclude unmeasured effects being achieved by the schemes, but on the basis of the results we could find no evidence of cost-effectiveness in term of prevention of reoffending.

Conclusion

The cost estimates presented here must be treated with some caution. Identifying and linking expenditure information to activity proved problematic and required a number of assumptions. One of the adult schemes received only one or two referrals at the time of the study and the other has changed over time. Moreover, it has not proved possible to identify the knock-on costs to other agencies in either case. Information about activities among the juvenile schemes was also very variable.

Factors associated with cost variations included employment status among adult offenders and gender and type of offence among juvenile offenders. While gender, of itself showed an inconsistent effect, the findings pointed to higher costs resulting from dealing with female violent offenders. This may be of some interest when planning services that incorporate a restorative justice element for juvenile offenders.

Our measure of outcome was based on reconvictions, which omits those offences that do not result in reconvictions. As a result the analysis is likely to be a conservative estimate of the underlying cost-effectiveness of schemes in preventing offending. Of the two adult schemes there was evidence that the West Yorkshire scheme was cost-effective in reducing further offending. In this scheme the proportion of offenders in the highest risk category that did not reoffend over the subsequent two years was relatively low. However, in terms of cost per prevented offences the evidence suggests this would appear to be the most cost-effective group to target.

Information was not available for all of the schemes but the evidence suggests that, while other, unmeasured outcomes may have been achieved, the juvenile schemes as they stood at the time of the study were not cost-effective in terms of reconviction.

Within the schemes the involvement of victims (where this occurred) tended to be associated with higher costs. However, the only scheme that routinely involved victims (West Yorkshire) was, for the most part, both lower cost and more effective than the other schemes.

7.   Conclusions and recommendations

Conclusions

As explained in Chapter 1, the research on which this report is based was undertaken at a time when most of the restorative justice schemes it examined were experiencing significant changes. Some, too, were experiencing major resourcing problems, and their levels of activity had declined significantly (one, indeed, had virtually 'closed down' at the time of our fieldwork). The 'prospective' element of the study, therefore, was considerably smaller in scale than originally planned, and based on relatively few current cases. On the other hand, the retrospective study of reconviction rates in the two adult schemes went largely as planned, and – although, as with all 'retrospective' research, the results must be treated with some caution – some interesting and encouraging findings emerged. These have also informed the cost-effectiveness element of the research, where some equally encouraging conclusions may be drawn.

The main conclusions of the study are listed under a number of general headings below. This is followed by some 'good practice' recommendations, based on the fieldwork at the seven schemes participating in the study and on the single visits to a further six schemes (and correspondence with a seventh).

Characteristics of the schemes studied

(a) Diversity

Schemes varied markedly in a number of respects. These included different understandings of the notion of 'restorative justice', variations in the amount and type of work they undertook with victims and differences in the types of offenders and offences dealt with. It is therefore not possible to draw definitive conclusions about the effectiveness or otherwise of 'restorative justice'; rather, conclusions may be drawn about particular schemes working in particular ways.

(b) Fragility

Although some schemes have survived for many years, the overall impression was one of fragility. Schemes were vulnerable to funding cuts and often dependent on work 'beyond the call of duty' by small numbers of exceptionally committed individuals. Mediation work also became a low priority for some agencies when faced with problems in meeting statutory requirements (a clear example being the transfer of probation staff from mediation to victim liaison work). As a result, numbers of referrals and interventions were often volatile from year to year.

(c) Levels and speed of intervention

Even at the times when they were receiving substantial numbers of referrals, most schemes made unambiguously 'restorative' interventions in relatively few cases. Direct ('face-to-face) mediation was, as a proportion of all the referrals identified, a rare event, and even 'shuttle diplomacy' tended to occur in only a minority of referred cases. This was largely because in some places victims were unwilling to take part in the process, but also (particularly in some of the more 'offender-oriented' schemes) because staff were reluctant to involve victims directly, preferring, for example, to persuade their young offenders to write letters of apology. As noted, these were not necessarily always delivered.

Cases also took a considerable time to complete (in one area, indeed, from initial contact to closure of the case could take over a year). It appears that restorative justice is a labour-intensive and time-consuming activity, with a great deal of preparatory and exploratory work – a significant proportion of which does not ultimately bear much fruit. This was partly the result of communication problems: unanswered letters and abortive visits to people who were out were commonplace. At the same time, though, a slow pace was actively encouraged in some schemes: "People need time to reflect on their feelings and the information they have been presented with. We do not hurry the process." scheme staff also pointed out that direct mediation has to be very carefully prepared, usually with several visits to both victim and offender before they are brought together. This applied even more forcefully to conferencing, which involved in some cases quite large numbers of participants. This situation raises some doubts about the future potential of mediation as a mainstream service capable of 'processing' large numbers of cases within (or outside) the criminal justice system.

Effectiveness

The effectiveness of the schemes was evaluated primarily through examinations of their *impacts*, their *outcomes* and their *cost-effectiveness*.

(a) Impacts

Downturns in activities in the schemes and a variety of practical difficulties made it impossible to interview as many offenders and victims as originally planned. We cannot therefore be confident that those interviewed are fully representative of all victims and offenders experiencing restorative justice in these schemes. In all, 23 victims and 43 offenders were interviewed during the research period.

Victims who had experienced some form of restorative justice were broadly favourable towards the concept. They appreciated the opportunity to "have their say", and some were pleased and even moved to receive letters of apology. Those who had not previously known their offenders often welcomed the provision of information about them, commenting that this gave them peace of mind. About two-thirds believed that the intervention had had some beneficial impact on the offender.

However, interviewees raised a number of concerns. In particular, some were sceptical about the motives of the offenders, and even of the schemes, feeling that the offender was "getting off lightly" and that they were being used to achieve a favourable sentence. Moreover, some victims found direct personal contact with their offenders unsettling and even intimidating. Offers of reparative work and of compensation were not generally well received. Finally, the most frequently cited negative aspect of involvement with the schemes was the time taken to complete the process.

The offenders interviewed were generally more content with the intervention in their case than were victims. They appeared to understand the purpose of the intervention and several commented that they welcomed the chance to say sorry. Over 85 per cent agreed that their own concerns had been listened to, and that they had been treated with respect. As might be expected, most had found the experience of meeting their victims embarrassing or upsetting, and in a small number of cases threatening. Despite this, most had found it in retrospect a more positive experience than they had expected.

Finally, although the sample was again not large enough for full confidence in the results, there were encouraging indications from the 'before and after' scores of the 28 juvenile offenders who completed CRIMEPICS II. These showed substantial improvements in attitudes towards victims and towards offending in general.

(b) Outcomes

As in many other areas covered by the Crime Reduction Programme, a key measure of the effectiveness of restorative justice schemes is their capacity to reduce reoffending, as judged by reconviction rates. We have accordingly focused on these in our analysis of outcomes in Chapter 6.

The retrospective study produced a very positive result in West Yorkshire, where a sample of offenders who took part in mediation did significantly better in terms of reconvictions than a comparable control group. They were also, as a group, convicted significantly less than predicted by OGRS 2.

The West Midlands results, however, did not support this finding, the intervention group doing no better than the control group when account was taken of previous offending. However, unlike in West Yorkshire, pre-court agreement to take part in mediation could be used by offenders in an attempt to persuade sentencers to pass a lower sentence, so it is possible that the West Midlands sample contained fewer offenders with a genuine desire to address their offending behaviour.

Finally, it is important to emphasise that many of the offenders dealt with by the West Yorkshire scheme had committed very serious offences: indeed, over half had received custodial sentences for the offence in relation to which mediation was undertaken, most of these being seen by scheme workers in prison. The fact that West Yorkshire was the only scheme in which a statistically significant outcome was found in terms of reducing reconviction, raises the distinct possibility that mediation works more effectively – and cost effectively (see below) – with "high tariff" cases than with more minor cases. This hypothesis certainly deserves further testing.

In the case of the three young offender schemes in respect of which we were able to compare intervention groups and control groups (Gloucestershire, Leicestershire and Suffolk), a few minor differences in outcomes were found, in most cases indicating that those who had received scheme interventions had 'done slightly better' than their counterparts. However, none of these differences were found to be significant (as measured by cautioning or reconviction rates); nor was there any strong evidence that the level of known offending might be reduced or the pattern of offences changed.[60]

Before leaving these conclusions, we should note that many of those who advocate wider use of restorative justice interventions do so because they see victims' satisfaction with such measures as being at least as important as reductions in reoffending. As their satisfaction with restorative justice would arguably be increased if reductions were achieved, the two measures are related. Victims' satisfaction is also arguably linked to crime reduction in that their increased confidence in the fairness of the system, as representing their interests as much as the offender's, may translate into behavioural change, such as a greater willingness to engage with the criminal justice personnel. Restorative justice may therefore have the potential to achieve more positive outcomes than traditional offender-focussed interventions. We were, however, unable to test these hypotheses on the basis of the research findings.

(c) Cost effectiveness

The evidence suggests that the West Yorkshire scheme is cost-effective. Moreover, although the proportion of offenders in the highest risk category who did not reoffend over the subsequent two years was relatively low, in terms of cost per prevented offences the evidence suggests this would appear to be the most cost-effective group to target.

Information was not available about outcomes for all of the juvenile schemes but the evidence suggests that, while other, unmeasured outcomes may have been achieved, the juvenile schemes as they stood at the time of the study were not cost-effective in terms of reconviction.

Within the schemes the involvement of victims (where this occurred) tended to be associated with higher costs. However, the only scheme that routinely involved victims (West Yorkshire) was, for the most part, both lower cost and more effective than the other schemes.

---

[60] We are not able to say whether, had their sample sizes been equivalent to those in West Yorkshire, the young offender schemes might not have produced statistically significant positive outcomes.

"Best practice" recommendations

Setting up schemes

We set out below, in bullet point form, the main recommendations to be drawn from this study. They are broadly subdivided under the headings used in Chapter 3. Where relevant, and in order to set them in a broader context, we cross-refer to the Youth Justice Board's *Draft Standards for Restorative Work with Victims and Young Offenders*.

Aims, organisation, staffing and training

● scheme aims and objectives should be clearly stated, properly documented and communicated to staff, clients and funding agencies. Practice should be monitored to ensure that it does not deviate from them. *(Draft Standards, 2)*

● schemes need clear and uncluttered lines of management and of accountability, avoiding over-elaborate structures. Managers should secure supportive and active participation by key representatives from other relevant agencies. *(Draft Standards, 1)* There must be regular reporting to line managers and scheme evaluation by those responsible for its day-to-day implementation.

● Managers should preferably have some background in youth justice, mediation or cognate fields. Schemes need to ensure that there is continuity in core personnel, recognising the limitations of reliance on single committed individuals.

● schemes should employ a co-ordinator to manage their day-to-day work. Co-ordinators' tasks will include logging referrals, assessment and allocation of casework, training and supervision of mediators and reporting to the scheme's management committee. A scheme should also ensure that it has sufficient secretarial or other support staff to assist with routine administration.

● Record keeping needs to be clear, accurate and complete. All interventions need to be accurately tracked and fully recorded. The data entry headings should be agreed and tested before the scheme takes its first referrals. Spreadsheets should be used from the outset so that data can be sorted for subsequent monitoring and evaluation.

● Volunteers are an asset, but need to be carefully selected and trained. They should be over 18, and police checks run on their application to participate. Schemes need to recognise that volunteers are not a 'free' resource: care must be taken to cost initial vetting procedures and subsequent training.

● All those who deal with victims or offenders must be appropriately trained. *(Draft Standards, 3)* Policies for initial and follow-up training must be fully planned and costed. Initial training should address mediation theory and practice, relevant legal considerations, and the scheme's own policies and administration. Training can be provided in-house (by experienced staff who are themselves qualified trainers) or by buying in from other schemes. Basic training needs to be followed up with a staff or volunteer development policy. This may include formal accreditation as mediators, the completion of educational qualifications, or development as trainers in their own right.

● On the job training, though valuable as a shadowing exercise for newly trained staff, should take place once basic training has been completed. Further training may be needs driven but should always address changes in the external conditions affecting practice; for example, changes in the law.

Referral criteria

● Referral criteria need to be derived from the scheme's aims and objectives. They should be clear and as comprehensive as possible. Schemes need to recognise that the wider the referral net, the greater the resource implications.

● Standard offender referral criteria should be clearly stated in a practice handbook. These should include such formal prerequisites as an admission of guilt, residence within the scheme's area, and a willingness to participate in intervention. Schemes may consider other factors such as the gravity of the offence, previous offending, the offender's response to any previous interventions, and any other relevant domestic circumstances.

● Care should be taken in the case of rape and other sexual offences, domestic violence and in racially motivated offences. Where shoplifting is concerned, clarity is required on the use of proxy or representative victims.

● schemes should consider how much individual discretion is to be given to those staff admitting offenders to its programme.

● schemes need to agree what information it wants about the offender and the victim they require from the referring agency.

Victim and offender protocols

● schemes should develop robust and transparent protocols for offender and victim contact. These should deal with the order in which contact is made, after what preliminaries, and subject to what conditions. *(Draft Standards, 4, 10)* Compliance should be routinely recorded and reviewed.

● The offender should be contacted first, and should be informed in appropriate language of the available interventions, including meeting the victim. *(Draft Standards, 5)* Young offenders in particular should be given the opportunity to talk through what happens in a face-to-face meeting with the victim.

- Victims should only be contacted once it is clear that the offender wishes to meet, to make reparation or in some other way to apologise. *(Draft Standards, 6)* Victims should not be pressurised into participating, nor be given the impression that they are somehow at fault where they decline to take part. Schemes should nevertheless aim to respond quickly once the victim has indicated willingness to participate. *(Draft Standards, 8)*

- The victim's wish not to be involved should be regarded as final, but not as affecting other aspects of any intervention applying to the offender.

Interventions

- There must be clarity in the scheme's intervention types and rigorous matching and following through on the intervention chosen in any case. Schemes should develop robust and transparent protocols for the conduct of the intervention. This includes the conduct of any meeting between the victim and offender, the participants' safety (including that of the facilitator or any others present), and the value given to the victim's preferences. *(Draft Statement, 11)*

- scheme managers need to set clear targets for the number of victims and offenders to be seen and the number of cases to be completed, as well as clear time limits both for the whole intervention cycle and its constituent stages. Time targets need to be realistically informed by resource constraints.

- Once agreed, meetings between victims and offenders should be conducted promptly. If one party withdraws, it is important that the other side is given the reason. Similarly, if the victim does not wish to meet an offender who is anxious to make direct amends, the reasons should be explained to the offender.

- Where victims are involved in either direct or indirect mediation, schemes must ensure that they are aware of what is to happen, the range of possible outcomes and are fully consenting. *(Draft Standards, 13)*

- Direct mediation should follow the established format in which each party speaks without interruption about the offence and the impact it has caused, responds to the other, asking questions and providing information, and makes a closing statement. *(Draft Standards, 15)*

- Care must also be taken that mediation procedures do not become formulaic. Both victims and offenders must perceive the procedures as valuing their contributions and as being responsive to their views. *(Draft Standards, 12, 16)*

- Neutral venues should always be chosen for direct mediation. In particular, victims should not be expected to meet their offenders in prison or at the offender's home. *(Draft Standards, 14)*

- Offenders for whom a meeting with the victim is likely to prove difficult may be encouraged instead to write a letter of apology. *(Draft Standards, 9)*

- Where letters of apology are the product of either direct or indirect mediation, the scheme must make clear to the victim whether they are to be put to any other use; for example, as mitigation.

- Letters of apology should be sent via the scheme, not directly to the victim. Schemes should scrutinise, but not amend them, even for grammatical or other minor reasons. A letter should not be forwarded if the scheme considers that it would hurt the victim.

- Offender interventions may usefully focus the offender's explanation for the offending; its impact on family relationships; victim awareness; future behaviour; substance abuse awareness and personal goals such as education and work. *(Draft Standards, 25)*

- Care should be taken about offers of reparation work or payment of compensation. Unfulfilled or unrealistic expectations seriously affect victims' satisfaction.

Closure, follow up, and evaluation

- schemes should ensure that they have appropriate procedures for closing the intervention, debriefing the parties and, possibly, thanking them for their participation, providing information on its impact, and obtaining feedback from the offender and victim. Feedback may be obtained by means of an evaluation form. *(Draft Standards, 21)*

- Whatever is agreed between the scheme, the offender and the victim, or between the scheme and the offender only, should be clearly written in everyday language and copied to all participants. *(Draft Standards, 17, 20)*

- Information on the immediate results of the intervention should not include responses to requests for longer-term access to details of the offender's behaviour, in particular, reoffending. *(Draft Standards, 22)*

- Research and evaluation needs to build in to any funding arrangement. This means that research requirements (e.g. PNC numbers for juvenile offenders) will comprise funding conditions. Evaluation needs to be large scale, and conducted a sufficient length of time following an intervention to accommodate reoffending data. Scheme co-operation must be a condition of any funding arrangements.

Appendix A   Summary of findings of the feasibility study

The feasibility study was carried out in the seven selected schemes between July and October 1999. The main findings were as follows:

(a)   The schemes varied considerably in the length of their operational life. Some had been very recently established; others had been in operation for up to 10 years or more. There was therefore considerable variation in their maturity, with some having undergone significant change in personnel and method.

(b)   There was also considerable variation in the number of offenders dealt with by the schemes. This was largely a product of their relative longevity, but also depended on referral turnover. Reoffending data could only usefully be generated in respect of the longer-established schemes, which included two of those dealing with young offenders, and the two dealing with adults.

(c)   Five of the schemes dealt only with young offenders. Of these, two (AMENDS, Mansfield) had particularly high ambitions and offered the potential for substantial evaluation of restorative justice activity. They had, however, been in operation for too short a time to generate an offender population to whom reoffending measures could validly be applied. By the same token, their numbers were small.

(d)   Two schemes dealt with adult offenders: West Midlands and West Yorkshire. Being long established, both offered substantial opportunity for retrospective analysis of reoffending. On the other hand, the major downturn in the work carried out by the West Midlands scheme precluded any evaluation during the main fieldwork.

(e)   The schemes varied in the point at which they intervened, and some intervened at more than one point. Some were caution plus or diversion schemes, others engaged in post-sentence mediation.

(f)   They also varied in the nature of the intervention. Some were ambitious, seeking to engage in a wide range of interventions; others were more modest both in aspiration and in practice.

(g)   Interventions in which the victim figures in some way varied from raising the offender's awareness of the harm caused, through writing letters of apology or explanation (which letters might not in fact be delivered to the victim), shuttle or go-between mediation (speaking to the offender and victim separately and reporting the other's views), to full face-to-face mediation. This last was however, achieved in only a small number of cases. Apart from the empirical research issue raised by this last point, an interesting theoretical question arises concerning what might be understood by the phrase, restorative justice.

(h)   Given these variations, confidence in the efficacy of these interventions, as a means of reducing reoffending, was not thought to be high. Even if we could demonstrate a lower than expected reoffending rate, for example, where the offender wrote a letter of apology, it would not necessarily be attributable to what might be unambiguously regarded as a restorative justice intervention.

(i)   Most schemes had been undergoing, or are about to undergo, internal change; typically, of personnel, practice, resourcing, number of referrals, institutional affiliation or status. Those dealing with young offenders had faced the arrival of YOTS, whose impact appeared in some instances to have diverted the schemes' energies in other directions.

(j)   schemes' paper records varied in comprehensiveness and detail. This was so both in the case of the administration of the schemes' referral and intervention practices, and in respect of income and expenditure. Gaps and inconsistencies were considered to be not conducive to confident analysis.

(k)   In all the schemes it was clear that the characteristics of the offence, the offender and (in some cases) the victim were likely to be associated with different levels of resource inputs. Although some applied a narrower range of interventions than others, it would not have been appropriate to assume a simple "cost per case" approach which simply divides total costs by activity in any of the schemes.

(l)   Resource data, in terms of numbers of visits and activities undertaken, was included on the retrospective files of most of the schemes and some indicated the number of hours involved. However, these data tended to be incomplete and dependent on who was recording the information. This information might have assisted us in predicting the cost for individual cases but it was thought unlikely that retrospective data could be relied on as the sole source of information about scheme inputs to the case.

Appendix B

Scheme descriptions

Introduction

This appendix comprises a basic picture of the seven schemes, including their origins and basic aims, the relationship between each scheme and the criminal justice system, their formal constitution and legal status, their training and recruitment practices, the source of their client base and their rules for selecting offenders and victims. It also looks at the range of intervention types employed. Descriptive material of this kind provides a sense of 'context' against which to interpret the results of quantitative analyses, and offers an opportunity to identify good practice and innovative ways of organising service delivery. At the end of each account, statistics are provided on referrals and completions.[61] We begin with the two schemes which deal with adult offenders.

Adult schemes

West Yorkshire

Origins, aims and objectives

Victim-offender services in West Yorkshire began in 1985, when the Leeds Mediation and Reparation Service (LMRS) was developed as one of the four original Home Office-funded experimental reparation projects[62] One of its main aims was to examine the validity of mediation/reparation as a way of working with high tariff offenders. In recognition of the importance of the work, funding of the LMRS was taken over by the West Yorkshire Probation Service in 1987 and over the next decade mediation work was developed across the county, with bases in Bradford, Calderdale and Kirklees/Wakefield. With the introduction and development of *Victim's Charter* work, the units became known as Victim-Offender Units.

In addition to their mediation work, the Units engage in *Victim's Charter* services (information to victims who have suffered a serious violent or sexual offence about the progress of the offender's sentence) and domestic violence pre-sentence reports. Whilst we are only concerned in this report with victim-offender mediation, it should be noted that the mediation work is a voluntary component competing with the pressure of statutory requirements of *Victim's Charter* services, the latter accounting for 90 per cent of the overall work of the units.

The principles of voluntarism, equality and choice are central to the philosophy of the West Yorkshire mediation service. Mediation is seen as a voluntary process of communication in which victims and offenders are offered a series of choices which they can accept or reject at any stage in the process. The evolving stages of the mediation process are viewed as a

---

[61] Where the statistics are stated as being collected over a particular period of years or months, the period includes the last named year or month.
[62] The others were Coventry, Wolverhampton and Carlisle.

continuum in which choice and empowerment are seen as essential to the process of resolving conflict, "denying victims and offenders all the options is to deny full empowerment and is against the principles of mediation" (Annual Report of Leeds Victim Offender Unit, 1997).

Accordingly, the process of mediation aims to provide victims and offenders with the opportunity to resolve conflicts, "within the wider context of the criminal justice system" with offenders having "a moral responsibility to put right, as far as possible, the effects of their offence" and victims having "a right to be involved in the process of criminal justice" (Annual Report of Leeds Victim Offender Unit, 1997).

Mediation is not, however, about forgiveness. The emphasis is on challenging offenders about their behaviour and providing victims with the opportunity to hear the answers to their questions, gain reassurance that the offence was not personal, and ultimately address their feelings and enable them to move on.

Organisation and funding

Although three of the units are located within probation service offices, victim-offender unit personnel are not trained probation officers. Lead management responsibility rests with one of the Assistant Chief Probation Officers (ACPO) and line management responsibility for each unit is with a Senior Probation Officer. The victim-offender units are managed by salaried co-ordinator(s) who are responsible for the day-to-day running of the units, budget management, assessment and allocation of casework, supervision of mediators and report writing. Several of the co-ordinators are actively involved in mediation or victim enquiry casework. Highly committed mediators who work on both a sessional and volunteer basis conduct the majority of this work.

There is little consistency of practice across West Yorkshire. Although it is a county-wide service, most of the individual units have developed their own distinct approaches. This applies to a range of issues, from the 'standard' letters giving information about the service, to the number of mediator hours allocated to each case, to the methods of record keeping and filing.

Staffing and training

Across West Yorkshire there are five co-ordinators and around 50 mediators, some of whom specialise in working with adult offenders or in specific offences (e.g. death by dangerous driving), and some of whom work with the range of offenders and offences.[63]

The co-ordinators and mediators working in the units reflect a broad range of ages (early twenties to mid sixties) and a wide spectrum of occupational backgrounds. Several indicated that their interest was related to their own experience as a victim of crime; some were motivated by a change of career, and others simply had spare time and were keen to be

---

[63] Following the introduction of fixed term contracts and age restrictions, the number of experienced mediators was drastically reduced with a number being ineligible or having resigned in protest.

involved in 'voluntary work with a challenge'. No formal qualifications are required, but the co-ordinators wanted mediators with 'people skills': good communication and rapport, empathy, inspiring confidence, non-judgemental and a degree of resilience.

Following an initial interview, there is a three-day training course. This covers such matters as the concept of mediation and its operational processes. Formal applications lead to a second interview. Subject to references and police checks, successful applicants are accredited by the West Yorkshire Probation Service to work as mediators.

Most mediators accompany or 'shadow' an experienced mediator before they are given a case as a primary mediator. There are significant differences in practice across the units: some new recruits accompany an experienced mediator for a limited number of cases, others may shadow for a number of months. Mediators attend regular meetings, which involves personal supervision with a co-ordinator. However, practice is not monitored, and one mediator voiced concern that the co-ordinators never actually witness the mediators in action.

Referral criteria and procedures

Referrals, which are 'offender led', can be taken at all stages – pre and post sentence – and can come from a variety of sources – primarily probation (90%), the police, social services and Victim Support. Conditions, which must be met, are safety for the participants, a willingness to take part and a guilty plea. Whilst referral to the Unit can be made at the PSR stage, no action can be taken until post sentence. This is seen as a further strength of the West Yorkshire mediation process: it is voluntary and has no influence on the offender's sentence. Whatever the other gains for the offender who participates, they do not include any reduction in sentence.

Once the offence has been subject to the criminal process, mediation is available to any offender and their identified victim(s). A significant proportion of cases involves serious offences and offenders with substantial prison sentences. However, offences in which there is considered to be a power imbalance are excluded. Prime among these are rape and other sexual offences. Likewise, caution is applied in cases of domestic violence and in racially motivated offences. There is, however, little standardisation of policy with regard to acceptance or rejection of cases referred and all the units operate on a slightly different basis. The Bradford unit, for example, does not deal with commercial crimes against large departmental stores, banks or building societies.

When a case is referred to the unit, the co-ordinator will read the case notes and allocate a mediator to make the initial assessment. The mediator will visit the offender, give information about the scheme, confirm willingness, and otherwise assess compliance with the referral criteria. If so, the victim will be visited and a similar process followed. If the criteria are not met no further action can be taken. This is classed as 'assessment only'. The assessment procedure is thus central to the mediation process and requires skill, judgement and experience; the main aim is to ensure that the offender is genuine.

Types of intervention

The unit offers both direct and indirect mediation. Direct mediation is a face-to-face meeting between victim and offender. Prior to the meeting (which is always held on neutral territory such as the probation office or prison if the offender is in custody), there will typically have been considerable preliminary negotiation; each party will have an idea of the questions that are to be asked. Direct mediation is a structured event in which the mediator acts as a facilitator between the victim and offender. There are basic rules and an established format:

- each party is allowed to speak without interruption about the offence and the impact it has caused

- each party is allowed to respond and to ask questions and to provide information

- each party is allowed to make a closing statement which acknowledges an understanding of the offence and the personal impact.

Both victim and offender will be visited about one week later to ask about their reflections on the process. The case is then closed.

In the case of indirect mediation, the mediator visits each party in turn and relays information about the other's feelings and the effects of the offence. Whilst this is sometimes referred to as shuttle mediation, the mediators see themselves as a 'go-between', attempting to facilitate a resolution to the conflict. With the information that the victim has provided the mediator will confront the offender with the effects of the offending behaviour. The mediator negotiates with both parties to attempt to reach agreement on an acceptable mediation outcome:

- the offender can write a letter of apology. The victim offender unit will decide whether the letter is to be sent; the letter is scrutinised to ensure that it does not re-victimise the victim. The letter is never sent directly to the victim, but is passed via the mediator

- the offender can make a verbal apology which is relayed to the victim by the mediator. The victim can acknowledge the offender's apology via the mediator

- the offender can voluntarily agree to pay some compensation

- the offender can voluntarily agree to do practical work either for the victim directly or for a third party (the community). The victim can suggest what practical work can be done.

Referrals and completions

It can be seen that direct (face-to-face) mediation is rare, only ten cases being recorded among 350 referrals. This was put down by staff to a combination of factors, including unwillingness by victims, the amount of time involved in setting up such meetings, and the fact that quite a high proportion of referred offenders in West Yorkshire serve prison sentences.

Table 31.West Yorkshire: summary of mediation statistics October 1999-March 2000[64]

Division	Referrals	Assessment	Information Only	Indirect Mediation	Direct Mediation
Bradford	32	15	0	24	2
Calderdale	29	11	2	8	1
Leeds	249	44	6	33	7
Kirklees	16	4	4	11	0
Wakefield	24	21	16	13	0
Totals	350	95	28	89	10

Offenders in custody pose particular challenges for the mediators; the mediator may have to confront the offender with difficult information and it largely rests on the skill and judgement of the individual case worker to present the issues in a way that is not counterproductive. It is recognised that offenders in custody may be particularly vulnerable and the prison probation officer and personal throughcare officer are routinely informed of any potential concerns after a mediation meeting. Other more practical difficulties may involve the resource implications of continuing with a case if an offender is moved to a prison outside the county, or situations where an offender appeals against sentence as considerations of the legal process outweigh the potential benefits of the mediation process.

Current developments

On 1 June 2000, the West Yorkshire Probation service announced that victim-offender mediation work was to have a reduced priority. This is largely because of the failure of the Service to meet national standards in Victim Enquiry work (Victim Charter cases should be referred within two months of sentence). Pressure to meet these requirements has resulted in the decision to limit victim-offender mediation work across all units.

West Midlands Victim Offender Unit

Origins, aims and objectives

The Coventry scheme opened in September 1985 as part of a Home Office pilot project. An undated document prepared for the Unit for Community Safety, Mediation and Reparation, West Midlands Probation Service, but current in July 2000, stated its aims and objectives as being related to working with offenders, victims and the community with the intention of reducing or preventing further offending.

More specifically, its aims include offering victims an opportunity to express feelings/views, to obtain information and also to demonstrate to victims that the Criminal Justice System has not forgotten them. In some cases communication with the offender can offer assistance in coming

---

[64] Source: West Yorkshire Probation Service, June 2000.

to terms with the offence and provide reassurance. Offenders are encouraged "to accept personal responsibility for their actions, to consider their victim and to make constructive use of opportunities for apologising, expressing feelings/views and for making amends".

Organisation and funding

For the first four years funding came from the Home Office and private sources; thereafter directly from the probation service. In 1989 it was wholly absorbed into the West Midlands Probation Service as an integral part of probation service provision, but with its own ring-fenced budget. Sister units were set up in Birmingham and Wolverhampton. The Coventry scheme became the Unit for Community Safety in 1993. It then employed a community safety officer and a volunteer organiser who also undertook mediation work. More staff were appointed with a commitment to community safety. Work expanded to include criminal work, neighbourhood mediation (referred from Housing Departments) and racial disputes.

In 1996 the ring-fenced mediation budget was distributed to provide mediation services across the county. Three main offices were set up. The first was in Coventry (moving to their current premises within the probation service in 1996), with two mediators, one project worker and the administrative assistant. The second, Wolverhampton, supported three part-time project officers and one administrative assistant. In Birmingham (1997) there was one full-time mediation officer and one part-time probation officer whose remit was to develop mediation.

Partnership schemes with funding from the probation service were set up in Sandwell (see Appendix D5) and Dudley, seconding probation workers and volunteers to handle mediation work. A third scheme in Walsall was unsuccessful and closed in March 2000.

Staffing and training

Staffing was very fluid over the years in the West Midlands. At one time the probation service employed four mediators across the three units, and sessional mediators and probation officers took on further cases. A County victim/offender development officer oversaw all activities. While she remains in post, there is relatively little mediation activity in any of the units and her time is taken up mainly with victim enquiry matters and the development of YOTS.

In the past there was minimal training for mediators. The present victim/offender development officer learned "on the job" and subsequently handled most training of any new staff. This involved a basic training course following which she accompanied new mediators for their first few cases. This co-working could continue for some time, depending on the nature of the case.

Referral procedures

The referral criteria were established in 1985 and published in internal documents that were current during the research period. The three main requirements were a guilty plea, an identifiable victim and a wish to take part. Offenders could be in any age group. Referrals came from one of seven sources:

- Youth Liaison Panel (young offenders on the threshold of prosecution)
- Youth Court
- Magistrates' Court
- Crown Court
- solicitor referral
- probation
- self-referral.

Referrals from the courts were usually made at the pre-sentence report (PSR) stage. In the case of the magistrates' courts and the Crown Court, referrals eventually became "automatic". Contrary to the first of the referral criteria, offenders would be referred even when they had not yet entered a plea. As one report noted, "should the defendant plead guilty, he is willing to apologise to his victim".

Where they were available in court for the purpose, mediators would identify offenders; alternatively probation officers referred the case automatically because they knew of the Unit's existence. Defendants would be asked whether they were willing to attend mediation in order to have a report to this effect included at sentencing. Doubtful cases were referred to the probation officer. In practice, assessment was superficial: the mediator accepted every case once it had been referred, and in the majority of cases wrote a report whether the offender (client) had been seen or not.

Types of intervention

The West Midlands service offered three types of intervention: mediation (direct, indirect and shuttle), reparation and compensation. The majority of adult cases in the years 1995 to 1997 comprised indirect mediation, if the victim was involved. In many cases the victim was not, due either to the lack of time between plea and sentence or because he or she was giving evidence. Letters of apology were often written; sometimes they were delivered to the victim, others remain on file.

Neither reparation nor compensation, which was once quite common, especially in cases involving youths and criminal damage, has been used recently.

A thematic inspection of victim contact work by HM Inspector of Probation at the beginning of 1999 came out well for practice and badly for management. This concluded that the sporadic mediation work that is currently undertaken is handled with care and real commitment, but the lack of proper management and funding, and the will to see the practice flourish, means resources are being squeezed and active mediation diminished. Some mediation continues in the partnership agencies (see above) but the probation service itself provides little to no mediation at all.

Referrals and completions

Table 32. West Midlands: all offender referral numbers 1996 to 1999

Year	Total number of referrals including juveniles
1996	103
1997	154
1998	90
1999	37

Referral practice was fraught with problems in latter years. There was a real lack of resources and management structure and an unwillingness to make any referrals. Only one mediator worked in the unit from 1997, who was expected to handle all referrals within the adjournment period. Inappropriate referrals were made, not adhering to the criteria upon which the practice was based.

It should be noted that because the purpose of the offender indicating a willingness to be involved with mediation was to record that fact in the PSR, a reduction in sentence was seen as an end in itself. In the majority of cases mediation was not subsequently pursued. Likewise, reports continued to be written for court use in the majority of cases, even where the client had not been seen at all. However, while the number of referrals during the mid 1990s was still relatively high, lack of personnel meant that clients could not be seen more than once. Table B3 below shows the number of adult referrals by court in the years 1995/97 (there is no entry for magistrates' courts in 1995 because the files have been destroyed). Table B4 shows the activity undertaken as a percentage of the number of referrals.

Table 33. West Midlands: adult offender referrals by court 1995 to 1997

Court	Year	Total number of adults referred	Client not seen	Client seen once	Client seen more than once	Report written for court
Crown	1995	59	17	26	16	32
Magistrates[65]	1996	29	9	8	12	13
Crown	1996	38	11	23	4	21
Magistrates	1997	52	26	6	20	26
Crown	1997	47	24	21	2	25

---

[65] There is no entry for magistrates' courts in 1995 because the files had been destroyed.

Table 34. West Midlands: activity as a percentage of the number of referrals

Year	Nothing done	Report written	Client seen more than once
1995	30%	57%	28%
1996	29%	51%	24%
1997	50%	54%	15%

Current developments

Although the scheme was virtually moribund at the time of our fieldwork, there have been recent signs of a revival and it is hoped that a new mediator will be appointed in Coventry in the Autumn of 2000. The local magistracy has also been showing renewed interest in restorative justice practices.

Juvenile schemes

The other five schemes studied dealt only with cases involving juvenile offenders (aged 10-17). All of these have been significantly affected by the introduction of multi-agency Offending Teams (YOTS) in early 2000, and in most cases their level of activity prior to this was greatly reduced owing to staff training and other preparations for the change. The following accounts relate principally to pre-YOTS practice, although some recent developments are also mentioned.

AMENDS (Waltham Forest Victim Offender Mediation Service)

Origins, aims and objectives

Waltham Forest Victim Offender Mediation Service, now known as AMENDS, was established in September 1997 as an unincorporated association having charitable status. It began with one part-time employee whose task was to develop and co-ordinate an independent mediation service. It took its first referrals in April 1998. During 2000 AMENDS established three further victim/offender mediation projects and became incorporated; it also manages a neighbourhood mediation scheme.

As stated in its statement of aims and objectives, AMENDS was established to provide a mediation service for the London Borough of Waltham Forest "to offer help to victims of crime to understand what has happened to them; and to help offenders understand and take responsibility for their actions". Other aims of the service include educating the public about the purpose and methods of mediation and, in particular, enabling the public to understand the nature of the causes of conflicts and the value of mediation as a means of resolving disputes peacefully. A further objective is to engage the local community in the activities of the service. Its staff consider the principles of restorative justice, including reparation, victim participation, offender accountability and re-acceptance within the community to be central. They also feel that the emphasis on reparation and the philosophy of restorative justice in general helps the service to work towards meeting its obligations under the Crime and Disorder Act 1998.

The scheme is an example of an independent model of mediation as distinct from those programmes organised by such agencies as probation, police or social services. Its staff believe that independence is best suited to deliver a service in which confidentiality and impartiality are core principles.

Organisation and funding

The major source of funding for the scheme is the Local Authority Social Services Department, whose contribution is matched by various Charitable Trusts. From April 2000, the scheme has also received SRB funding. AMENDS has always been and continues to be involved in extensive fundraising.

AMENDS is governed by a management committee, which includes advisors drawn from the police, youth services, social services and community safety partnerships. Their position as trustees means that they act in a private capacity. Its manager is the original part- (since October 1998, full-) time employee. Her main responsibilities include management and business areas, service development, finance and fundraising, and direct supervision of co-ordinators. The manager has legal qualifications, training and experience of mediation and family group conferencing and has worked for the voluntary sector. She is also responsible for managing four other AMENDS mediation schemes.

AMENDS also employs a full-time co-ordinator to run the Waltham Forest Mediation Service who has been in post since September 1999. The co-ordinator's responsibilities include case management, providing volunteer support, arranging and delivering training to the volunteers, and providing a link with other agencies in the borough. Waltham Forest service also has an administrator (employed since January 2000) who has responsibility for all administrative tasks in the office, but must also be able to deputise for the co-ordinator.

Staffing and training

A principal feature of the service is its reliance on volunteer mediators. In common with the co-ordinator and the administrator, they undertake visits to offenders and victims, and conduct mediations. From a base of 11 in 1997, there are now 34 volunteer mediators recruited from – and representative of the ethnic mix of – the local community.

AMENDS has an open recruitment policy, which includes those who have 'spent' criminal convictions. Volunteers must be over 18 years. While some have relevant experience through involvement with Victim Support, community or neighbourhood mediation and counselling, no specific qualifications are required. Applicants are sent a recruitment pack and are invited to attend a training course. Upon completion the service assesses the individual, follows up references, arranges a police check and holds a post-training interview. Successful applicants have a probationary six months and their first three mediations are conducted with a senior mediator. Some of the volunteers assist with administrative work in the office.

The co-ordinator is a retired police officer. The administrator has a degree in psychology and has undertaken training in counselling. Since being in post, they have each attended a number of courses related to their roles, including the five day Thames Valley Police Restorative Justice Conferencing course (see Appendix D). More generally, AMENDS now runs its own in-house training; in particular that designed for the volunteers. This lasts for the equivalent of four days. Sessions cover a variety of topics, including what mediation is and the role of the mediator, the youth justice system, restorative justice, developing listening skills and styles of conflict resolution. AMENDS' referral system and protocols for mediation are explained, along with case administration and writing of visit report forms. Reliance is placed on role-plays to act out and work through each stage of the mediation process. Thereafter, volunteers have monthly support meetings and are given the opportunity for ongoing training.

AMENDS has recently completed a training manual for mediators. This sets out the protocols to be used with offenders and victims during the mediation process. It also contains protocols on equal opportunities and anti-discriminatory practices.

Referral criteria and procedures

Referrals to the service began in April 1998 and from then, until late 1999, the majority came from the local borough multi-agency cautioning panel comprising representatives of the police, probation, education, youth justice and, on rare occasions, Victim Support. The panel met weekly, undertaking a risk assessment that attempted to obtain a holistic picture of the young person, including the risk of reoffending, the history and nature of the offence and family circumstances. The panel ceased activity in late 1999 when the local Youth Offending Team (YOT) was established. The latter now provides the majority of referrals (currently about five a week). There have been some initial problems with these referrals; victim details have been difficult to obtain and there is a lack of information about ethnic origin that AMENDS uses to complete its ethnic monitoring.

The scheme deals primarily with minor offences of criminal damage, theft (in particular, shop theft), handling stolen goods, burglary, assault and criminal deception. Excluded are homicide, racially or sexually motivated offences, domestic violence, aggravated assaults, armed robbery, drugs offences and possession of offensive weapons. Racially motivated offences were also excluded during the research period but AMENDS is starting to deal with such offences.

There are two categories of referral criteria. The first, which further differentiates offender and victim criteria, is objective:

The young person:

- must be aged 10 to 17 years and have committed an offence
- must have admitted guilt (and formal proceedings in the case must be concluded)
- must be resident in Waltham Forest (this a requirement for Local Authority funding)
- must show signs of remorse

The victim:

- must be identifiable (the service will conduct mediations with corporate bodies but they must identify a representative victim, for example in cases of shoplifting)
- does not have to be resident in Waltham Forest but if he/she is normally resident outside the borough, the service needs to weigh up the costs of undertaking the mediation.

A young person who meets these criteria is then assessed at an initial meeting with a mediator, in which the following, more subjective, criteria are applied (similar considerations are applied in the first meeting with any victim):

- a willingness to participate in mediation;
- suitability for mediation (offender is remorseful; victim is receptive to mediation);
- that it would be safe to carry out a mediation; and
- the ability and capacity to take part in mediation process.

The use of volunteers has at times caused practical difficulties. In particular, it can sometimes take up to four weeks for an initial home visit to be organised as the volunteers try to arrange a mutually suitable appointment time.

Once a referral is accepted, two mediators are allocated to the case, as far as possible reflecting between them the social characteristics of the victim and the offender. Brief details of the case are given to the mediator and a letter explaining mediation and stating a date and time for a home visit is sent to the young person and his/her parents/guardian. During the home visit, the mediators explore with the young person and the parents what mediation is and how it works, discuss the nature and background of the offence, look at safety elements and explore whether the young person is remorseful, and whether open to mediation and reparation. Mediators should complete a visit report form and an equal opportunities monitoring form. If the young person is not willing to participate in mediation then the process will stop at this point, or, indeed, at any subsequent stage.

Where the offender is willing to proceed with mediation, the victim is contacted by letter or telephone. If a victim is visited, the mediators should complete a visit report, and an equal opportunities form. The mediators likewise explain the nature and role of mediation and explore whether he/she is open to receiving reparation. Much time can be spent scheduling home visits and mediations; the whole process can take from four weeks to three/four months. It is also important to note that over half of the victims AMENDS deals with are corporate.

Types of intervention

Intervention can take the form of simply the initial home visit, a series of visits, a letter of apology, a verbal apology or a face-to-face meeting.

Where direct mediation is deemed suitable, the venue will be on neutral ground, save in cases of shoplifting, where the face-to-face meeting has often occurred at the store premises. Each party is supposed to have approximately three meetings each before the face-to-face meeting. While recognised as a key aspect of the process, some of the corporate victims interviewed only saw the mediators for a few minutes before going into the meeting. Some of this group said that they were not sure what was expected of them and what might happen in the meeting.

When the meeting is completed, an agreement form is filled in where applicable. Types of agreement may include an apology, handshake or restitution of goods and money. Any agreement reached by the parties is entirely voluntary; it is not enforceable at law.

Mediators debrief each party and encourage the victim and offender to complete an evaluation form. The mediators themselves complete a direct mediation report form and send the parties a copy of the agreement, if applicable.

Where direct mediation is considered to be unsuitable or the parties do not wish to take part, indirect mediation will be offered. This may be a letter of apology or a spoken apology conveyed by the mediators to the victim. In the case of both direct and indirect mediation, offenders and victims are asked to complete evaluation forms and a letter acknowledging their courage in participating is sent to them. In many cases reviewed evaluation forms were not completed. Also, some of the offenders interviewed did not appear to have received a proper debriefing at the end of the process. In one instance where the victim had failed to keep the appointment the offender indicated that she had not been given the opportunity to explore the reasons why, and consequently remained confused and very disappointed about the process.

Referrals and completions

The majority of referrals are of young people aged 14 to 16 who have been given a reprimand or final warning, although priority is given to final warnings and then reprimands with risk factors identified. The following tables show firstly the number of offender referrals between April 1998 and April 2000 and, secondly, summarise biographical and offence details between January and March 2000.

Table 35. AMENDS: offender referral numbers April 1998 to April 2000

Year	Number of referrals
April – December 1998 1999 January – April 2000 Total	74 185 69 328

Table 36. AMENDS: summary of offender biographical and offence details January – March 2000

Year	January – March 2000 (57 referrals)
Gender	Male 70%; Female 30%
Age	10 years (4%); 12 years (1%); 13 years (26%); 14 years (30%); 15 years (19%); 16 years (11%); 17 years (9%)
Ethnic group	Not known (52%); White British (21%); Asian (9%); Mixed Race (6%); Black British (4%); Black African (4%); Bosnian (2%); Polish (2%)
Main offence	Shoplifting (37%); Criminal damage (23%); Theft (14%); Assault (9%); ABH (7%); TDA (4%); Non residential burglary (2%); Handling stolen goods (2%); Attempted deception (2%)
Referral type	Reprimands (88%); Final Warnings (12%)

As outlined above, it is only since the beginning of 2000 that the scheme has had a full-time co-ordinator and an administrator. The scheme was also relocated during the period of the research. For most of the time before this, AMENDS had only one paid part-time staff member and 11 volunteers, many of who were inexperienced at victim-offender mediation and required the co-ordinator to accompany them on home visits and mediation work. AMENDS was a new project and the co-ordinator had a variety of tasks beyond case management, including developing the project, recruiting and supervising volunteers and securing funding. In the first half of 2000 it expanded its volunteer base to well over 30. It is therefore appropriate to consider the figures on interventions in two parts.

Table 37. AMENDS: referral outcomes April 1998 – December 1999 (n= 259); January – April 2000 (n=69)

Division	Referrals	Direct mediation	Written apology	Spoken apology	Offender home visit
1998-9	259	6	12	4	16
2000	69	1	6	4	18
Totals	328	7	18	8	34

Current developments

- The service (paid staff only) is now also involved in running group sessions on victim awareness/empathy for those on the local YOT Final Warning programme.

- The scheme is also starting to work on the new court orders, such as action plans and reparation orders.

- Both of these developments will mean that the types of offences AMENDS works with will expand, including more serious offences. Also, there will be a departure from their traditional way of working in that they will be involved with the process at the pre-sentence stage.

- As a result of working on court orders, priority will be given to the orders before final warnings. They have now developed a practice that, for most reprimand referrals (unless high risk factors attached), they will send out a letter offering the service of meditation and put the onus on the offender and his/her parent/carer to contact them.

- AMENDS will be recruiting soon for their next round of training in September/October 2000. Further, they will need to provide training for their current volunteers on working with these new court orders.

- AMENDS offer Personal Safety Training (run by the local police) for all female volunteers. They are hoping to extend this to include male volunteers.

- In partnership with a postgraduate student from Middlesex University they are developing a set of factsheets for young offenders that will examine the effects of a range of offences on victims.

- AMENDS is to pilot a new victim/offender mediation database that has been developed from the one used by their neighbourhood mediation service.

- AMENDS in partnership with Waltham Forest College is developing an accreditation course in Mediation (covering both theory and practice) which will be offered at the college from October 2000.

Gloucestershire Diversion Unit

Origins, aims and objectives

The Gloucestershire Diversion Unit has its origins in a 1993/94 pilot scheme which was sparked by a visit to the Northampton scheme (see Appendix D). The impetus for the present unit, which formally commenced work in November 1997, was the Audit Commission's 1996 paper *Misspent Youth*. There is no direct connection between the present scheme and the 1993/94 pilot, save in some of the key personnel who were appointed at that time. The initiative has developed as a result of a collaborative approach to youth crime prevention in Gloucestershire reinforced by continuing review. In October 1999 the unit moved from County Council premises to offices above a police station in Gloucester. Its location is not significant to service delivery, as clients rarely attend at the unit itself.

Gloucestershire Diversion Unit is an inter-agency partnership initiative aiming to "service the community by contributing to a reduction in youth crime and the harm and fear caused by it". For the offender, this is achieved by "the provision of individually tailored programmes which provide an opportunity to make reparation for individual offences"; for the victim, "the Diversion Unit provides victims with a place to express their needs and to positively and constructively address some of the fear, anger and upset which they may be left feeling after an offence has taken place".

The unit seeks to make its aims and objectives "consistent with the stress on restorative justice underpinning the youth justice reforms contained in the Crime and Disorder Act 1998 as well as with the statutory principal aim introduced by that legislation".

Organisation and funding

The Unit is a multi-disciplinary team seconded from social services, police and education. There is a management structure comprising a Chief Officer Steering Group, a management board and a unit manager. The Steering Group includes chief officers of police, county council, social services and probation. The management board comprises managers from all the partnership agencies (Victim Support, police, county council, voluntary sector, social services, education, youth service and probation.). A unit manager leads the diversion team itself.

The unit became part of the YOT management structure in April 2000, though it remains self-contained. The unit manager has remained in post, but is now answerable to the head of YOT. Other services within YOT increase the options available to the unit, and facilitate communication. From the outset, the unit was prepared for the transfer into the YOT, which has taken place with minimal disruption to the unit itself.

Core funding for the unit has been provided by the lead statutory partner agencies, primarily Gloucestershire County Council and Gloucestershire Constabulary. A range of independent grant-making trusts and charities has funded specific areas of project work. Some of the charitable funding has expired and has not been renewed. The introduction of YOT, which requires core funding for the unit, significantly alters these earlier arrangements. Seconded staff continue to be paid by their respective agencies.

Staffing and training

There are four categories of staff. Diversion officers (initially four, now five) are seconded from the social services, education and the police to work in the unit for two to three years. One social services post has become permanent. Family Group Conference Coordinators are employed solely for this purpose and are paid per session. Because the workload has not justified appointment to the original figure of 12, the number of coordinators remains at three. For the same reason, the ten recruited volunteers have seldom been called upon. They are now part of a mentoring scheme developed as a partnership between the YOT and the Youth and Community Service supported by a grant from the Youth Justice Board. Fourthly, there is one part-time administrator who works 19 hours per week.

The Diversion officers bring their own expertise to the unit. They have minimal training (mainly observing and shadowing other diversion officers) prior to handling their own caseload. Further training, sometimes by experienced members of other schemes, is possible; attendance depends on the individual's need for the course, availability and funding. Officers undergo regular supervision by the unit manager. There has also been a substantial pre-YOT training. The Family Group Conference Co-ordinators meet monthly to discuss conferences, invite outside speakers from relevant organisations (e.g. drugs projects), and have attended a two-day course run by the Hampton Trust. The Co-ordinators feel they have learnt most from each other and from their own experiences. The volunteers were trained by the unit manager and a colleague on a course which ran for six consecutive evenings.

Referral criteria and procedures

Until the introduction of YOT, referrals came via the Youth Offending Review Group (YORG) – a multi-agency panel comprising a representative from each of the police, education, probation, youth justice team and the Diversion Unit. All young persons admitting guilt were referred to YORG, which made the decision whether to refer the offender to the unit or to prosecute. That decision was itself informed by an assessment made by the unit on the offender's suitability for intervention. This assessment had to be completed by a diversion officer within three weeks of the referral, following which YORG either approved the action plan or recommended prosecution. If approved, the plan is returned to the officer for implementation. In the year ended 1998, 80 per cent of cases referred from YORG to the unit resulted in an action plan.

Referral criteria have normally been based on the caution criteria, with some flexibility. This is considered important when dealing with young people, but has occasionally resulted in inconsistent and from time to time, inappropriate referrals.

All young offenders referred by YORG for assessment will be seen at least once by one of the diversion officers, whereupon a decision will be made whether to involve the victim of the offence. The unit will only contact the victim if the officer believes the victim will benefit in some way; for example, where the offender has agreed to apologise, or to meet the victim. There is some inconsistency here, not only in the making of the decision whether or not to contact a victim, but also in the method chosen. There is a practice handbook containing intervention guidelines, but each officer makes an individual decision about the case and proceeds as he or she sees fit.

Types of intervention

Intervention may assume one of the following six forms: mediation; reparation; compensation; retail theft initiative; reducing reoffending and family group conferencing (FGC). Whatever form of intervention is followed, each officer, if appropriate, usually undertakes with the offender at least one session on peer pressure, victim awareness, career planning, drugs therapy and offence awareness.

Mediation involves an arrangement "where the offender and victim can meet face-to-face in a supervised session or communicate by letter or video to consider the offence and its impact on the victim or community". It thus contemplates both direct mediation and indirect mediation, which includes letters of apology.

Compensation involves payment directly to the victim, reparation involves a commitment whereby "the offender can directly repair any damage caused or engage in practical work indirectly for a nominal third party or charity".

The retail theft initiative, in which "the Diversion Unit is working alongside the local retail and business community to develop practice which seeks to address retail theft by young people", has been more successful with some stores than others. In some stores the diversion officers and their clients are welcomed by senior personnel who take time to talk to the young person and explain the effects of the theft on the store, its staff and customers. Others, despite encouraging noises, fail to find the time for such meetings.

Reducing reoffending is "an individual programme which would also identify any factors which may help to reduce the risk of a young person reoffending. The Diversion Unit works in collaboration with a wide range of agencies and communities to implement action plans which may relate to school, work or training, health, family relationships and personal development". Thus may include courses on drug use or fire setting.

"The Diversion Unit can co-ordinate a family group conference to bring about a plan for the resolution of an offence. This process puts the family and young person at the forefront of the decision-making process". The FGC project targets the most serious offences referred to the unit — dwelling house burglaries. It is a more intensive and interventionist model than the mainstream process. With separate funding for this work there have to date been 12 conferences; recent referrals have been negligible. Success is also limited. The majority of the young people reoffended soon after their conference, but FGC co-ordinators believe there were positive elements which resulted from the conferences, and their success should not be measured in terms of reoffending alone.

Referrals and completions

In its first year of operation (November 1997- October 1998) the unit received 144 referrals; in its second year (November 1998- October 1999), 145. The tables below summarise, first, biographical and offence details of those referred in the first year of operation, and, second, initial responses made by victims and offenders to proposed interventions, and completion rates achieved by the unit in its first year of operation.

Table 38. Gloucestershire: summary of offender biographical and offence details 1997- 1998

Gender	73% male; 27% female
Ethnic group	96% white
Main offence	Shoplifting 28%; Theft 12%; Criminal damage 11%; TWOC 5%; Burglary (dwelling) 4%; Burglary (non dwelling) 2%; Others 8%

Table 39. Gloucestershire: summary of initial responses made by victims and offenders to proposed interventions, and completion rates achieved by the Unit in 1997- 98

Initial response of young person	Unc-operative 10%; Co-operative 87%
Initial response of victim	Unco-operative or not willing to take part 33%
Work completed by DU	Co-operative and willing to take part 66%
	Direct mediation (including retail) 33%; Indirect mediation 22%; Letter of apology 28%; Reparation to victim 4%; Reparation to community 3%; Financial compensation 9.5%

Current developments

Since the introduction of YOT in April 2000 there have been significant changes to the Gloucestershire Diversion Unit

- a further administrative assistant has been employed to cope with a vastly increased workload

- the number of referrals has risen significantly

- another diversion officer has been seconded from social services

- referrals now come via final warnings

- contact with the young person must be made within five days of referral

- assessment of the case must be made within two weeks

- officers visit the young person at home, make an assessment then complete the Assett document, calling on other agencies for information as required

- cases should be completed within three months, although this is not a hard and fast rule

- contact with victims remains much the same, but there are issues of data protection to be resolved arising from the Crime and Disorder Act's direction to "share" information

- officers believe that the calibre of clients has changed- they seem more entrenched in their criminal careers. One girl recently said she could not understand why she was suddenly getting all this attention just for stealing some shampoo, when she had been stealing cars for years!

- YORG has been disbanded.

Leicestershire Young Offenders Diversion Scheme

Origins, aims and objectives

As its name suggests, this is principally a diversion scheme, rather than a mediation scheme. The initial impetus for its creation was the guidance in Home Office Circular 14/1985 on the cautioning of offenders. The first step was the creation in July 1987 of a pilot multi-agency Juvenile Review Panel. In appropriate cases the Panel offered young offenders who were to be cautioned by the police the alternative of participating in various intervention activities. Its success led to the formalisation of the multi-agency panel. A scheme Co-ordinator (now scheme Manager), with administrative support, was appointed in 1990, and the jurisdiction of the renamed "Leicestershire Young Offenders Diversion scheme" (YODS) was expanded county-wide.

Further changes occurred in 1993 when the voluntary agency which had been providing the intervention activities found itself unable to maintain its assistance in response to the scheme's increasing caseload. The decision was taken to establish an in-house pool of volunteers, led by a Volunteer Co-ordinator. The scheme has operated under this structure until the changes introduced by the Youth Offending Teams (YOTs).

Its current statement of aims and objectives adopts the police case disposal policy which prioritises the following two 'objectives':

- to develop clear and consistent cautioning, diversion and prosecution criteria which emphasise the nature of the offence, the characteristics and antecedents of the offender and which take account of the effect of offending on victims as well as public interest factors

- to ensure that quality decision-making is made at the earliest opportunity and lowest appropriate level for all offenders by police decision-makers

These might be seen more as a set of procedural goals than an overarching mission statement. In support of the 'objectives' is a lengthy list of 'aims' which include a commitment to divert appropriate cases from the formal criminal justice system, to achieve a reduction in recidivism, the speedy and fair processing of cases, and, more recently, the incorporation into the service delivery of "the victim's views".

There were, however, some noticeable differences between these aims and objectives and those contained in the volunteers' information pack. Few of those interviewed could confidently describe the scheme's specific aims, in particular in terms of outcomes. They could give abstract assessments of their perceptions of successful (or unsuccessful) cases, which typically stressed the importance of vaguer concepts such as 'connecting' and 'communicating' with the young offender, but placed little emphasis on a reduction in reoffending.

Organisation and funding

The Youth Offending Committee (the original Chief Officers' steering group), which includes the Chief Constable, Chief Executive, Chief Probation Officer, Chief Crown Prosecutor, Community Safety Officer and the Directors of the Social Services and Education Departments and the Leicestershire Health Authority) retains a broad oversight function, "to oversee strategic criminal justice issues at chief officer level".

Reporting to the steering group is an executive group of Assistant Chief Officers, now known as the "Young Offenders Co-ordinating Management Group". This group, which includes Assistant Chief Officers from the Police, Social Services Department and the Probation Service, Community Safety Officers from the City and County Councils, a Magistrates' Clerk and a representative of the Crown Prosecution Service, is said to have responsibility for managing the expenditure of YODS and for ensuring a co-ordinated approach to youth justice in Leicestershire. It is unclear how the latter function is achieved and how it is distinguishable from that of the Chief Officers' group.

Day-to-day operations are supervised by the "Diversion scheme Management Group" comprising middle managers of the participating agencies which meets the scheme manager quarterly. A full-time staff of four undertakes administration and co-ordination: the scheme manager, the interventions manager, an administrative assistant and a clerical assistant. The scheme manager, in addition to holding overall responsibility for daily operations, is also concerned with staff recruitment and training and was chair of the weekly meeting of the two multi-agency Diversion Panels (one for Leicestershire City and one for Leicestershire County) until the Panel's decision-making function was absorbed by the YOT.

Funding during the early stages was provided by the participating agencies, both directly and through the secondment of staff and provision of premises. A financial review in 1995 consolidated funding arrangements within the Social Services Department, now relocated as a result of the Crime and Disorder Act 1998 within the Chief Executive's Department. About one-third of the funding is provided by Leicestershire Constabulary, and another third by social services; the other main contributor being Leicestershire Probation Service.

The organisational hierarchy in relation to YODS seems top-heavy for what is a limited initiative operating within a relatively small budget. Over-inclusive, and at the same time vaguely defined, supervisory responsibilities appear to be blurring the scheme's once simply stated goals.

Staffing and training

Apart from the full time staff of four, the scheme depends on a 61-strong group of volunteers, of whom 48 were active at the time of the research. They come from a wide range of backgrounds, the majority being recruited through the city and county volunteer bureaux or the Probation Service volunteer training scheme, or by word-of-mouth. Most were white females (77%); the interventions manager commented upon the difficulty of attracting ethnic minority and male volunteers (who represent 11% and 20%, respectively, of the total).[66]

All volunteers attend an induction training course of four, once weekly sessions each lasting two to three hours. Here "the basics" are covered: including an overview of the scheme, techniques and protocols for dealing with young people and the scheme's administrative requirements. There is a follow-up interview with the interventions Manager for the purpose of the volunteer's formal registration with the scheme.

The provision of adequate support for volunteers, in terms of both training and ongoing supervision, was a high priority. On going training, including the monthly overview sessions, appeared to account for a substantial proportion of the managers' workload. Their purpose was to introduce a variety of more specific relevant issues and subjects (e.g. child protection, drug/alcohol education and self-esteem). The scheme staff felt that the quality of the training,

---

[66] While the scarcity of male volunteers was seen as a national problem, the anager expressed more specific concerns about the difficulties of recruiting and retaining ethnic minority volunteers. The practice of conducting home visits during early evening hours was a significant deterrent to Asian female volunteers, some of whom had withdrawn from the scheme as a result. She also felt that the scheme's close association with the police might be deterring black people from volunteering because of distrust of the police among those communities.

for which certificates are issued upon completion, made the scheme attractive to the volunteers. This was reflected in the comments of the volunteers themselves, four of whom saw the scheme as a stepping stone in their career development.

The scheme also operates a support system for its volunteers. A small group of the more experienced volunteers take on the role of Volunteer Support Worker (VSW). For reasons of health and safety, as well as to monitor quality of service delivery, VSWs accompany the volunteer to the first meeting with the young person.

Referral criteria and procedures

Typically, referrals were made to the Diversion Panel by the police, but were sometimes made by CPS. Because of its good relationship with the scheme, CPS usually returned cases which had mistakenly gone through for prosecution. In 1998, the majority of offenders referred were white (90%) males (78%) aged 15 to 16 years (43%).

When a young person was arrested, the police assessed and scored the case using formal criteria based on the gravity of the offence (from one (least) to five (most) serious). An offender who had admitted guilt and was assessed at levels three or four was referred for a Panel decision. Prior to the meeting, case files were assembled by the scheme administration staff who gather information, as necessary, from the offender's school, Social Services and other relevant agencies. The files were then sent to the Police Panel representative (an Inspector) for advance reading. The Inspector presents the file to the other Panel members at the following meeting.

Various factors were taken into account during Panel decision-making, including the offender's age, previous offending, the gravity of the offence, response to any previous intervention work, contact with any other support agencies, and any significant social factors (such as family bereavement or other difficult circumstances). The strength of the multi-agency approach was easily observable during the Panel meetings. A majority decision was taken on each case. The choices open to the Panel were to:

- return the case to the police for a Caution or Formal Warning (level four)

- give a Panel Caution (with the offer of intervention work with a volunteer (level three)

- send the case for prosecution (level four)

- take no further action.

Table 40 gives a breakdown of the decisions taken by the Panel on all cases referred to the scheme during 1998.

Where a Panel Caution was to be administered, an initial judgement was made as to the most appropriate intervention work that might be offered. This could be renegotiated with the offender at the caution or even later at the contract meeting with the volunteer if necessary.

Table 40. Leicestershire: panel decisions on referrals, 1998

Panel Decision	Number of cases	Percentage of total
No further action	15	4%
Police caution	63	17%
Written panel caution	16	4%
Panel caution	191	51%
Prosecution	88	24%
Total	373	100%

Following the decision to administer a Panel Caution, the offender was formally requested by the scheme manager to attend, with his/her parent/guardian, the local Police Station to receive a caution from a police sergeant or inspector. Separate leaflets for offenders and parents were provided, containing information about the scheme and contact details for further information. A Panel member also attended the caution to explain the intervention process (including its voluntary nature) and the activity options available, and to secure the offender's agreement (or not) to participate. About half the 'Panel cautioned' offenders rejected the intervention offer at the caution. The manager explained that this was usually because other support was already being provided or because steps were already in place to confront reoffending.

Following the caution, the Interventions Manager holds an Allocations Meeting with the VSWs to allocate the offender to a volunteer worker. Once allocated, a letter is sent to the parent/guardian of the offender setting an appointment for the volunteer and VSW to visit and to convene the intervention. This approach is thought to be an effective means of both reinforcing the volunteers' association with the scheme, an agency of 'authority', while simultaneously creating a distance from the authority presented by the police.

Types of intervention

Work packs covering such topics as anger management, assertiveness training, peer pressure, victim awareness and the consequences and implications of offending had been developed in-house. Community reparation work was also facilitated, for example safety information packs have been filled for the Fire Brigade, litter cleared from public areas, and gardens sometimes tended. Helping young people to explore employment opportunities was popular as was helping them to become involved in local leisure activities (such as attending youth or sports clubs).

Almost every intervention undertaken included a session to work on the consequences and implications of offending. When asked if this exercise contained a victim awareness component the scheme managers said that the details of service delivery were left to the volunteers, but that victim work was "under-developed". Some of the volunteers said they routinely addressed the victim's perspective while others said they allowed the offender to lead.

It was not uncommon for offenders to write letters of apology to their victims. These were usually sent by the scheme to the victim, but responses were seldom received.

Managers and volunteers alike expressed reservations about taking a more substantially restorative approach in their work. In particular they had concerns about the use of group conferencing for the types of young offenders constituting their caseload. The general feeling was that it was a heavy-handed approach for what were relatively minor offences, and harsh on what were relatively young offenders. They were also deeply concerned about the implications and potential for negative impact on victims. Victim work seemed to influence the scheme in a diffuse way which can best be described as a generally raised awareness of the issues which formed part of the perspective brought to an essentially offender-centred service, rather than constituting a specific focus.

Referrals and completions

During 1999, a total of 274 offenders were referred to the Diversion Panel continuing a decline from a peak of 540 referrals made in 1995. Table 41, which shows the number of cases referred and the number and percentage of those receiving Panel Cautions and interventions, confirms that while an increasing proportion of referred cases have been receiving Panel Cautions, still only half of referrals receive this outcome and even fewer have ever agreed to undertake intervention work with a volunteer.

Table 41. Leicestershire: referral numbers and outcomes 1994- 2000

Year	No. of cases referred to the scheme	No. (%) of referred cases receiving Panel Cautions	No. (%) of referred cases agreeing to intervention
1994	516	N/A	47 (9%)
1995	540	215 (40%)	87 (16%)
1996	423	200 (47%)	99 (23%)
1997	376	184 (49%)	121 (32%)
1998	373	191 (51%)	109 (29%)
1999	274	139 (51%)	116 (42%)
2000[67]	79	47 (59%)	31 (39%)

There were no reliable data available on drop-out rates from intervention work. A review of the scheme's completed files (end 1998) for the reconviction element of this project suggested that a substantial minority of offenders do not complete the agreed intervention. Nevertheless, such cases are often recorded as successful completions: these assessments appeared to be influenced by the quality of the relationship between the volunteer and the offender. The notion of success, especially amongst the volunteers, centred more on engaging with the offender, rather than with a reduction in reoffending. In the assessment of an unsuccessful case, for example, a volunteer observed: "Someone that didn't engage at all – not turning up – because

---

[67] Includes cases referred between 1 January and 30 April after which the Diversion Panel was disbanded.

something positive can come out of every meeting with the young person. If one thing that someone said in the police station has an impact or something a parent of volunteer says as a result of all this process going on sinks in and makes a young person think, then that's a success."

Failed cases which were acknowledged as such seemed to be those in which the offender became unwilling or uncommunicative during the intervention, i.e. those who did not keep appointments with the volunteer or refused to co-operate during sessions. Offenders who simply expressed their wish to withdraw, or stated that they had already derived enough benefit from the contact, or did not wish to pursue agreed activities seemed more likely to be recorded as having had a successful outcome.

Current developments

The scheme now focuses on the provision of short-term interventions for young offenders who are referred by YOTs. The scheme's trained volunteers continue to undertake interventions with the young offenders as they did before, under the supervision of the Interventions Manager who is responsible for their recruitment and management.

Mansfield Restorative Conferencing Programme

Origins, aims and objectives

This programme, which commenced work in May 1998, drew its inspiration from the growing political interest in victims, the general thrust of policy development through the Crime and Disorder Act 1998 and more particularly the Mansfield Crime Audit (Crime Concern 1991-1992). It was to a large extent modelled on the Thames Valley Police initiative (see Appendix D).

Mansfield Division was chosen as the pilot site within Nottinghamshire Police, receiving its first case referrals in July 1998. Some four months later, and informed by an internal evaluation of client satisfaction, group conferencing was extended to Bassetlaw, and eight months later, to the Newark and Worksop Division. The Bassetlaw YOT became fully functional in July 2000 following a review in Mansfield which indicated high levels of satisfaction among victims, offenders and multi-agency partners.

The Mansfield scheme operates against the background of the *"Divisional Policy. Restorative Justice – Reprimands and Final Warnings"* issued by the Chief Superintendent on 26 August 1999 and, as its senior manager informally explained, in keeping in particular with the second of the six principles and objectives of the Youth Justice Board: "confronting young offenders with the consequences of their offending for themselves and their family, their victims and the community and helping them to develop a sense of personal responsibility".

Organisation and funding

The programme appeared to have no coherent or effective management structure. Managerial responsibilities for the programme's implementation, development and day-to-day operations seemed to have been added to the existing workloads of three police officers: the Chief Inspector heading the Community Safety Department, who, as an Inspector within the Mansfield Youth Justice Team, had initiated the conferencing programme. The Chief Inspector's senior management responsibilities included the advancement of the Force's youth justice work; specifically, this included the development of the YOT's and management of policy development, implementation and training requirements for the Restorative Group Conferencing programme. While control shifted to YOT on 1 April 2000, the senior manager retains line management responsibilities for both that and restorative conferencing.

Delivery of the conferencing programme was co-ordinated by one of the middle manager sergeants who, until the full implementation of the YOT, had directed a team of approximately eight police officers who officiated at the conferences. In addition to his regular duties as a Beat Manager Sergeant, the co-ordinator was responsible for allocating referrals and for general administrative duties in relation to conferences. He also facilitated some conferences himself and much of his time has been dedicated to training facilitators, both within and outside Mansfield Police. The specific role of the other middle manager sergeant was more difficult to discern. Described as "working full-time in the Community Safety Department on youth justice", it did not appear that he had undertaken any administrative duties for the programme. The supervisory staff responsible for the authorisation of cautioning was familiar with the aims of the restorative practices being pursued.

The weaknesses of its management structure were evidenced in the programme's slow progress and in the comments of the police officers tasked with facilitating conferences. It appeared never to have progressed past the initial unsettled phase typical of new initiatives to develop into a coherent and stable implementation. Since its beginnings, practice has been erratic: in December 1998, seven months after its introduction, the programme stopped taking referrals. The senior manager explained that this was because no protocol had been established which could pass confidential victim information to the co-operating agencies involved in YOTs. Conferencing did not begin again until May 1999. Practice was again apparently affected by the extended absence during early 2000 of the programme's co-ordinator who was seconded to provide conferencing training to other police services. Although his duties were reassigned during that time there was, nonetheless, a reduction in the conferencing caseload while he was absent; only ten cases were referred between the beginning of December 1999 and the end of March 2000. Of these ten referrals only four resulted in full conferences.

There is no dedicated funding for this scheme. At its inception, two small grants (£5,000 each) from the Single Regeneration Budget were allocated, together with an additional £5,000 from the County Council. Much of this was spent on initial and follow-up training and certification as restorative conferencing trainers and on "various administrative costs". £5,000 has been earmarked for a programme evaluation, which has yet to be carried out.

Despite the absence of core funding, its hidden costs belie the senior manager's characterisation of the scheme as a "shoestring" operation. Substantial unspecified resources were being consumed in the form of police officers' time in the often protracted preparations which precede any conference, and the support provided by two police sergeants, one of whom was assigned to the labour-intensive co-ordinating role. In a failed funding application made by the senior manager in November 1999 this last was estimated at £74,000 over three years. The co-ordinator has since been relieved of these duties by the YOT.

Staffing and training

The programme is delivered by Conference Facilitators, most of who were Beat Managers who assumed this function in addition to their regular duties. At the time of the fieldwork there were 20 officers trained as facilitators in Mansfield (a further 12 in the Newark and Worksop Division), and three of these had undergone further training to become Conferencing Facilitator trainers.

Three one-week residential training courses had been run since the programme's introduction. The first two were presented by Thames Valley Police which has produced a comprehensive curriculum for the promotion of their model of restorative conferencing (see Appendix D). The bulk of the training materials present a practical and highly prescriptive guide to running restorative conferences. Without exception the facilitators lauded the quality of the training they had received, generally describing its effect as inspiring. Included on the courses were several representatives of other statutory agencies (including probation, social services and education). Their presence encouraged the officers to take a broader outlook on how they should deal with young offenders. However, the need to adapt to these agencies' working practices created the potential for confusion in the officers' understanding of their responsibilities for the programme. The training provided by the Thames Valley police seems to have generated a disproportionate focus on equipping officers to facilitate conferences without offering guidance to managers in the establishment of a cohesive structure within which to run the programme.

Referral criteria and procedures

The scheme covered young offenders (10 to 17 years) who had committed a cautionable offence. Typical were assault, theft (shoplifting), criminal damage, public order offences and car-related crimes.

A Divisional Policy protocol for referring cases for restorative conferencing was issued in 1999, together with feedback and evaluation forms. The protocol provided for referrals to proceed through one of two routes depending on the offender's criminal record. If the offender had been cautioned previously and admitted guilt to the current offence, a 'Final Warning' could be administered through a restorative group conference. First offenders would usually receive a restorative 'First Reprimand' (or Caution) unless the victim wished to meet the offender, in which instance the case would also be taken to a restorative group conference.

The facilitators were responsible for assessing cases allocated to them. This involved contacting and visiting victims and offenders and any other relevant parties in the case to explain the conference format and to set a date for it to be held.

Conferences were run according to a standard script. Facilitators explained that the preparation work in advance of the conference was crucial. During conferences the facilitators complete the conferencing paperwork, including the formal cautioning of offenders. Many of those interviewed felt that these tasks, when coupled with the time-consuming nature of the preparatory home visits, were burdensome.

Types of intervention

Most of the conferences resulted in a face-to-face apology. If victims did not attend and a restorative caution was given, letters of apology were sometimes written by offenders, both to the victim/s and to the offender's parent/s. There were several instances of offenders apologising to victims in person during a conference and also being required to write letters of apology to them.

Although one of the YJB's principles, to which Mansfield's programme subscribes, encourages "reparation to victims by young offenders" (Youth Justice Board, 1999), this was not usually facilitated because police insurance was said not to cover such interventions. Financial compensation to victims was also sometimes agreed although not always subsequently paid as there was no means of enforcing the agreements made.

Referrals and completions

Between July 1998 and April 2000, 68 cases (involving approximately 132 offenders) had been referred to the programme. Of these, only 17 (25%) restorative conferences (attended by a victim) had resulted. The vast majority of the remainder had led to a restorative caution which was typically delivered by a Police Inspector with only the offender and members of his/her family in attendance.

Various reasons were given for the small proportion of cases resulting in a full conference. For example, victims sometimes declined to participate and it sometimes proved difficult to reach mutually convenient dates for those involved (especially in cases involving more than one offender or victim). It seemed that for many of the types of offences for which juveniles were being arrested, conferencing was inappropriate or an excessive response to the offence. In the case of shoplifting, the absence of a direct or easily identifiable victim proved problematic. Reliance on proxy victims (shop manager or security guard) made several of the facilitators uneasy.

While some facilitators wanted more discretion in deciding which cases to run as full conferences, others were concerned that it would leave unchecked the temptation to "cherry-pick" cases. They reasoned that in selecting the cases most likely to succeed in conferences there was a risk of neglecting the more difficult cases which might be least likely to respond in the conference setting but were most vulnerable to reoffending and therefore most in need of attention.

The facilitators' target for completing conferences from referral date was two weeks; it appeared that this was seldom achieved. However, once completed, as an internal evaluation conducted in 1998 showed, the greater majority of those who had taken part in restorative cautioning were either "satisfied" or "very satisfied" with the process.

Current developments

Several of the facilitators felt that while the programme was operated without a dedicated administrator, it was at risk of losing momentum. Although the senior manager explained that the restorative conferencing programme had, since the advent of YOTs, established a "more settled structure now", interviews with the facilitators undertaken between March and May revealed a lack of awareness of procedural changes within the programme and of how referrals and conferencing would be affected by the YOTs. While the programme's prolonged teething problems may not have been helped by their implementation and the practice changes that YOTs have entailed, the programme's erratic progress cannot be explained only by their advent.

There remains a need for general awareness-raising regarding restorative justice practices. When asked about the process of referral by investigating officers, the senior manager regretted that potential referrals were sometimes not made because, as one facilitator above had suggested, restorative justice was yet to become embedded in police procedures and culture. However, there did not seem to be a strategy to address this problem other than the now out-dated statement of Divisional Policy on reprimands and final warnings, which specified the restorative cautioning procedure.

Suffolk County Council (Youth Justice) Caution Plus Scheme

Origins, aims and objectives

As in Leicestershire, the scheme studied in Suffolk was not primarily engaged in mediation work, but in general 'caution plus' interventions with young people. Caution plus was established in Suffolk as part of the county's overall response to the duty placed on the local authority by the Children Act 1989 to "take reasonable steps designed to encourage juveniles within its area not to commit offences, and to reduce the need to bring criminal proceedings against juveniles in the area". It additionally responded to Home Office Circular 59/1990, which recognised the utility of cautioning young offenders. Caution plus was introduced throughout Suffolk in 1992. The three schemes were based on the experience of a programme that had been operating in the west of the county since 1988 and of a pilot scheme in South Suffolk initiated in July 1991. The schemes were located in South Suffolk (Ipswich), West Suffolk (Bury St Edmunds) and North Suffolk (Lowestoft).

The aim was to engage young offenders in a programme of work, designed for them as individuals, addressing the context of their offending behaviour and helping them to recognise the impact of their offending on victims and the community. A further aim was to identify strategies that would enable the young person to avoid reoffending. The scheme also provided the opportunity for such other agencies as education and health to assist the young person. "By attending a caution plus programme, there is an opportunity to address offending behaviour at an early stage. In this way the caution plus scheme has an educative role in helping the young offender to recognise and understand the consequences of further offending on other people and himself/herself."

Caution plus was presented to young offenders as a positive alternative to going to court. They were made aware that prosecution would have been seriously considered in their case and that the scheme offered them a final chance to alter their behaviour. Caution plus was replaced by Final Warnings on 1 June 2000.

Organisation and funding

Until the end of August 1999, NCH Action for Children (in partnership with Suffolk Social Services) managed and provided all youth justice services, including caution plus, for North and West Suffolk areas. In South Suffolk these were all run by Suffolk Social Services. Despite some common principles and aims, the practice of caution plus both at referral and intervention stage appears at times to have differed between the schemes.

From September 1999, caution plus has been funded by Suffolk County Council and overseen by the newly formed Suffolk Youth Offending Team (YOT), although it continues to be administered locally by members of the YOT in each of the three areas. There also continue to be variations in practice, though the main aims and objectives of the caution plus programme appear consistent.

A co-ordinator within YOT division organised and ran the caution plus programme in that area. The sessions with the young person were conducted by the co-ordinator and at times by such other members as the education welfare officer, drugs counsellor or probation officer. In South and North Suffolk, sessional workers were also occasionally employed to undertake the one-to-one work.

Staffing and training

During the fieldwork, the co-ordinators in the three areas were police officers, each of whom had experience of working with young people. No specific qualifications were required for the sessional workers, but they tended to be people with an interest in youth work.

Materials including safety guidelines, ground rules and procedures were distributed to the newly recruited sessional workers, and sometimes, a training evening was held, but in most cases, initial training prior to taking sessions appeared minimal. Primary training comprised shadowing those more experienced during the conduct of a session with a young person.

The initial training for the co-ordinators was very similar. Following their appointment, they attended the Youth Justice Board training run by Thames Valley Police on Final Warnings and Restorative Justice (see Appendix D). All co-ordinators expressed the view that their police training should be supplemented by training specific to their new role.

Referral criteria and procedures

Caution plus in Suffolk was available for young offenders aged between 10 and 17 years, the majority of offenders being between 14 and 16 years of age. Offences commonly dealt with included criminal damage, theft (including shoplifting), handling stolen goods, burglary, common assault, ABH and minor incidents of arson. Although intended for those who had been considered apt for prosecution, caution plus was available for those borderline cases where a decision had been made not to prosecute but some form of intervention was believed necessary to accompany a caution.

The process was as follows: referral; consideration by the Youth Liaison Committee; home assessment visit; and direct intervention. The majority of referrals came from the Police Administration Support Unit in the local areas. Referrals were sent to the youth justice teams each week for discussion in the Youth Liaison Committee (YLC). Introduced in 1990 and formerly known as Juvenile Liaison Committee, YLC was a multi-agency panel comprising representatives from the police, probation service, education welfare department and the youth justice team.

At the YLC meeting the police representative outlined the details of each referral, the others sharing any further information; the purpose was to agree how to deal with each young offender. The options included 'no further action' (although this was rare), caution, caution plus or prosecution. Decisions were based on the criteria set out in the police's Prosecution and Diversion Manuals. Where the caution plus criteria were met, the referral was usually held over to the next meeting to enable the co-ordinator to assess the young person's suitability for an intervention by means of a home visit.

Where the YLC agreed that caution plus might be appropriate, in most cases a home visit would be conducted by the co-ordinator to assess the offender's suitability for the programme. The visit is proposed in a letter to the offender's parent/guardian, usually with an explanatory leaflet.

During the visit the co-ordinator discusses a number of matters concerning the offence and the young person's education and life history. Where appropriate, details of the proposed intervention would be signed by the participants, subject to a final decision being taken by the police at the subsequent YLC meeting. Approval of a caution plus intervention was recorded in the case file, designated as 'awaiting allocation'.

The attitudes of those who attended the YLC seemed to be essential in the decision-making process. The number of referred young offenders that were recommended for caution plus programmes appeared to depend on how fully the panel favoured diversion from prosecution and what types of offences the panel considered appropriate for diversion. Those offered caution plus tended to have one or more previous cautions.

Types of intervention

A caution plus programme normally comprised four to six one-hour sessions held on a one-to-one basis with the co-ordinator or a sessional worker. The venue might be the scheme office, the young person's home, a café or other public place, school or a police station. On some occasions group sessions, for example with prison officers, have been included.

The content of the session was specified in the agreement made during the home visit, designed to meet the needs of the young person. Despite this individuation, the programme had common aims and objectives. The sessions typically included:

- offence-based work (the details of the offence and the young person's excuses/reasons for the behaviour)

- focus on the family network and the effects of the offence on those relationships

- victim awareness/empathy work (victims of crime in general and particular, and the impact of the offence on them)

- focus on the likely future of the young person should reoffending occur

- focus on the needs/interests of the young person (education/training/leisure activities, all aimed at encouraging a different non-offending lifestyle).

During each session the young person would usually complete worksheets or questionnaires based on these various matters. Where appropriate, sessions would also involve such other agencies as education, welfare, community drug teams, the fire service and the prison service.

While the scheme was designed to incorporate reparation to the victim or community, practice was variable. In the Southern division victim reparation extended no further than the writing of a letter of apology, not always delivered. Greater emphasis on reparation work is evident in the other two areas. The practice of letter writing was more common, as was such community reparative work as picking up litter, gardening, visiting the elderly and other voluntary work. There were, however, very few cases of direct reparation to the victim. Latterly indirect reparation declined as relevant organisations became increasingly reluctant to work with young people because of health and safety issues and it became difficult to find people to supervise the reparative work.

Referrals and completions

From a number of Annual Reports and discussions with case workers, it appears that in South Suffolk approximately 20 to 25 per cent of all cases discussed at the YLC resulted in a referral being recommended for caution plus (seeB12). Records have not been complete enough and figures have not been forthcoming to detail for all years in the three Suffolk divisions the total number of referrals to the YLC and then how many of those resulted in recommended referrals for caution plus. However, it seems probable that West and North Suffolk divisions would have had a similar rate of referral to caution plus.

Table 42. South Suffolk: referrals resulting in caution plus recommendations

Year	No. of young offenders referred to YLC	No. of referrals accepted for caution plus
1995	294	64
1996	369	74

From discussions with caseworkers in West Suffolk, it would seem that most young people recommended for caution plus completed the programme. Data from South Suffolk (which is incomplete at times) would suggest that overall about two out of three young people completed caution plus.

Table 43. West Suffolk: completion figures for caution plus

Year	No. of completed caution plus cases
1992	25
1993	45
1994	51
1995	81
1996	77
1997	61
1998	64
1999 (Jan-Sept)	30
Oct 1999-May 2000	31

It would seem probable that North Suffolk would have had similar completion rates but figures were not available.

Table 44. South Suffolk: completion figures for caution plus

Year	No. of cases referred for caution plus	No. of completed caution plus cases
1992	57	42
1993 (July-Dec)	32	18 (8 ongoing)
1994	57	30 (9 ongoing)
1995	64	53
1996	74	45
1997	Not available	Not available
1998 (July-Dec)	13	10
1999	Not available	26
2000 (Jan-May)	Not available	17

Current developments

● The Youth Liaison Committee will not form part of the referral process under final warnings: this is generally regarded as a loss by those who worked in caution plus.

● Some of the caution plus worksheets/questionnaires will still be used in final warning programmes.

● One of the main differences will be the length of the intervention: final warnings can be a maximum of three months, whereas caution plus was seen as a short intervention.

● Another difference is the required emphasis on victim involvement under final warnings.

Appendix C

Estimation of costs

This appendix describes the estimation of costs for each of the schemes. Throughout the term *fixed costs* has been used for those costs that were necessary to have been incurred for the cases to be processed but have not been linked to individual variations in input levels to those cases. These costs have been allocated on the basis of the overall level of scheme activity and therefore tend to be very dependent on the degree to which stand alone schemes operate at capacity.

West Yorkshire

The work takes place in four divisions. In each a co-ordinator (salaried manager) is responsible for allocation of referrals and for supervision of sessional mediators. Sessional mediators are employed on a casual basis to carry out all subsequent activities involving offender(s) and victim(s).

Costs were calculated for cases for which there was full information as follows:

- £142 (referral and other activities).
- plus number of co-ordinator hours * unit cost.
- plus number of sessional mediator hours * unit cost.
- plus volunteer expenses on a divisional basis.
- plus staff expenses on a divisional basis.

Where information was not available the cost was predicted using:

- the overall average number of sessional mediator hours (8.33 hours)
- 2.38 hours if unemployed, 42 minutes if employed and 1.85 hours if there was no information.

The costs for the sample (including prospective cases) are shown in tables C1 and C2 below.

Table 45. Predicted and observed costs (£)

Cost definition	N	Mean	Median	Max	Min
Observed costs	39	347	347	651	199
Predicted costs for intervention group	154	300	283	384	237
Observed costs with predicted costs where observed costs were not available	177	296	276	651	199

Table 46. Predicted and observed costs by division

Division		Observed costs	Predicted costs for intervention group	Observed costs and predicted costs for all cases[68]
Bradford	Mean	N/A	278	277
	N	0	35	42
	Std. Deviation	N/A	10.3	10.6
Calderdale	Mean	204	300	284
	N	3	15	18
	Std. Deviation	1.8	30.7	46.2
Leeds	Mean	199	278	278
	N	1	68	78
	Std. Deviation	N/A	11.8	19.6
Wakefield	Mean	363	363.23	358
	N	35	36	39
	Std. Deviation	75.4	29.8	74.0
Total	Mean	347	300	296
	N	39	154	177
	Std. Deviation	86.7	40.6	51.9

[68] All cases includes the prospective cases for which information was available and those cases for which outcome data were not available.

West Midlands Victim Offender Unit

Costs were based on information provided about the staffing levels and salaries and accommodation used in 1995 to 96, the main year from which retrospective cases have been taken. Four people were involved in the scheme: the unit manager, two mediators, and an administrative assistant. The administrative assistant worked half time on mediation related work. Together the manager and administrator added £8.22 to the hourly unit cost of a mediator. This gives a total hourly cost of a mediator of £23.32 (1998 to 99 price levels).

The unit manager estimated that each case took between 12 and 15 hours. This results in the estimated cost of a case lying between £280 and £350, with a mid-point of £315 at 1998 to 99 price levels.

There is some concern that this estimate does not allow for the costs of those cases where the intervention was minimal. Case files over a number of years indicated that 30 per cent of all cases had 'no action' of any kind, and a further five per cent involved some action, such as a phone call, or letter written to court, but no work with the offender. From her records, the unit manager estimated that the number of cases handled in 1995- 96 was 132, although there were concerns that this figure was too low. Other sources of information were no longer available. If we assume that 65 per cent of the 132 cases had significant activities taking place the cost per case rises to £500.

AMENDS

From January 2000, the AMENDS scheme had a full-time manager, a full-time co-ordinator and a full-time administrator. The prospective case costs were estimated on the basis of:

- managerial input (including direct supervision, management committee and steering group (£48 per case)
- caseworker time spent on organising case work and supporting volunteers (£148 per case)
- YOT worker input to the referral process (£23 per case)
- cost of cases where no contact made with offender (£10 per case)
- administrator time on general administration (£54 per case)
- training and recruitment costs of volunteers (£50 per case)
- number of administrator hours* unit cost
- number of volunteer hours* unit cost of sessional worker.

Fixed costs are very sensitive to assumptions about the number of cases dealt with by the scheme, information that was difficult to establish with much confidence because of the scheme's rapid development. Estimates shown are based on the assumption of 96 cases per year, reflecting the level of activity at the time of the prospective study generalised to an annual figure.

There was some police input in five of the cases, social worker involvement in four cases, a drugs worker and educational welfare officer input to two cases. Levels of input were not high generally – at most these professionals were involved in a meeting with the offender. There did not appear to be any referral on for other interventions.

Overall average costs were £422 for the cases where there had been some active involvement. Should the scheme manage to increase activity to estimated full capacity of 240 cases per year costs would drop to £257 for the cases where there had been active involvement. If we did not cost the volunteer input the average cost per case drops to £354.

Gloucestershire Diversion Unit

Estimation of costs of cases

One manager and three practitioners staffed the unit at the time of the research (all working full-time for the unit). The three diversion officers had different agency backgrounds and were seconded on a one-year basis (with the option of a second year). One was an education welfare officer, one a police officer and one a social worker. Although it was a policy decision to take a multi-disciplinary approach to staffing the unit, the actual work was carried out on a generic basis, and for this reason a generic unit cost was calculated for a diversion officer (averaging out details of individual pay and conditions). The manager (a trained social worker) was employed directly. Clerical support was supplied on an ad hoc basis: the unit had access to a word processing facility at the County Council. The manager estimated that the unit's work would have occupied a clerical worker for 2.5 days per week, so a suitable amount has been added to the unit costs of the manager and diversion officer.

Fixed costs for this scheme included the referral and review after initial assessment by the YORG group (£5 on each occasion), team meeting (£30 on each occasion) and management input to the scheme (£80 per case). Together this brought the fixed costs to £70 + £80 per case. The costs of prospective cases (23) were based on these plus diversion officer, management and other professional time multiplied by their respective unit costs. Retrospective case costs were based on:

- fixed costs of referral and review (£150 per case)
- management input to the scheme (£80 per case)
- average direct management input to cases (£2 per case)
- average level of other professional input (£28 per case)

- cost of cases assessed as unsuitable (£44 per case)
- predicted diversion officer costs (£49+(£46*number of visits)).

The average cost of the 21 prospective cases where there had been an intervention was £392. The predicted cost for these cases excluding the allocation of costs of cases assessed as unsuitable was £395. Including all of the factors in the above formula the predicted costs for these cases was £439 and for retrospective cases £452.

Family Group Conferencing

Family Group Conferencing (FGC) in Gloucester received funding from a voluntary organisation and handled all cases of domestic burglary. Family group co-ordinators set up a conference with relevant parties (offenders' and victims' families, relevant professionals etc.). Four family co-ordinators were available and were paid £12 per hour for their involvement. Details were supplied of the actual FGCs held during 1998 (seven) and 1999 (six).

Table 47. Gloucestershire: cost of Family Group Conferencing 1998[69]

	Total	Per case
Staff hours	252	36
Worker cost	£3,0273	£434
Miles travelled	1,110	159
Travel cost	£396	£57
Additional FGC costs (supplies)	£319	£46
Staff hours spent in meetings	23.5	3.4
Worker cost of meetings	£282	£40
Miles travelled to meetings	344	49
Travel costs associated with meetings	£123	£18
Staff hours spent in training	62	9
Worker cost of training	£747	£107
Miles travelled to training	208	30
Travel costs associated with training	£74	£11
Total cost of FGC	£4,968	£712

[69] Figures may not add exactly due to rounding.

Table 48. Gloucestershire: cost of Family Group Conferencing 1999[70]

	Total	Per case
Staff hours	168	28
Worker cost	£2,013	£336
Miles travelled	1,087	181
Travel cost	£395	£66
Additional FGC costs (supplies)	£173	£29
Staff hours spent in meetings	55	9
Worker cost of meetings	£660	£110
Miles travelled to meetings	301	50
Travel costs associated with meetings	£109	£18
Staff hours spent in training	0	0
Worker cost of training	£0	£0
Miles travelled to training	0	0
Travel costs associated with training	£0	£0
Total cost of FGC	£3,350	£558

Leicestershire Young Offenders Diversion Scheme

At the time the research was carried out, there were four people involved: scheme manager, interventions manager, administrative assistant and clerical assistant. (Details relate to arrangements and process before the changes brought about by the introduction of Youth Offending Teams.) All staff work full-time and exclusively for the scheme.

Fixed costs for this scheme included a panel meeting costing £80 per case. Fifty five per cent of cases had a panel related outcome-panel caution, written or verbal. Verbal caution cases were offered an intervention. Allocating all the costs onto those that generated a panel outcome resulted in £144 per case. Other fixed costs included the action meeting and subsequent administration (£24) and £147 for volunteer training and support. For prospective cases and those retrospective cases where information was known the cost per case was estimated on the basis of these fixed costs and the time spent by scheme and intervention managers, the administrator and volunteers multiplied by the appropriate unit cost.

There was quite a high input of non-scheme staff on the retrospective data set but prospective data indicated that virtually all involvement by non-scheme staff was through the panel meeting and action meeting. The only other involvement recorded was for one case where the scheme initiated a referral/activity with a social worker (plus 10 minutes actual contact time) and educational social worker.

---

[70] Figures may not add exactly due to rounding.

The model for predicting management hours where information was not available used violence and gender. One other significant predictor, knowing the victim, was not independently associated with inputs, as all those who were convicted of a violent crime knew the victim. Female violence was associated with the highest input and female non-violence with the lowest.

The only predictor for volunteer hours was the information collected about type of contact. As would be expected less time was spent on those who had just a preliminary interview than those with more interviews. Highest input was to those cases where the offender undertook some type of community work.

Retrospective cases where input was known (108) were estimated to involve less than one hour of management time but prospective cases (13), which were not different in terms of case characteristics, involved close to three hours management input. The difference was attributed to systematic underestimates retrospectively. As a result, recorded and predicted management inputs were inflated by 2.9 to reflect this difference. Similarly, volunteer hours spent on prospective cases were on average 9.6 hours, compared with five hours estimated for retrospective cases. The administrator input was closer to an hour per case than the average of 35 minutes estimated retrospectively.

Once the adjustments had been made to the time input and the predicted costs using sessional worker hourly rates to reflect volunteer input, the average cost per case was £406 per case. Costs were just £334 per case when these were excluded.

Mansfield Restorative Conferencing Programme

The costs estimated below are all underestimates as detailed information was not available about some inputs[71] and it was not possible to allocate the costs of cases where no intervention took place. However, the information does provide an indication of the types of activities and likely direct costs associated with these.

The co-ordinator (police sergeant) spent approximately eight hours per week on administration duties for the programme and supervision of facilitators. On the basis of 51 cases being processed in eight months (that is 1.75 cases per week assuming there are 29.3 working weeks in eight months once annual leave is taken into consideration) the fixed cost of administration and supervision was estimated as £121 per case. No information was supplied about prospective cases but examples of types of cases that had been dealt with and estimated levels of input were provided to the costs researcher.

Example 1: Group conference.

This would involve two or more individual meetings with scheme staff, discussing victim awareness and general offending behaviour. In this case there were two victims; children's home employees.

---

[71] For example, travel time appears to have been excluded and there is not enough information for us to estimate the costs of all participants in all conferences.

- Total preparation time on case was three hours (£67).

- Group conference lasted 50 minutes. Facilitator cost (£19). Others attending: offender, two victims, two children's home representatives, and foster carer. Children's home reps costed as social workers (£38). Total cost of conference (£57).

- Outcome – referred (or recommended) to anger management counsellor. No details of costs available.

Total cost of case including administration cost (see above): £245.

Example 2: Preliminary interview only.

Offender re-offended before completing scheme activities. One offender, one victim. No contact by scheme with victim.

- Preparation and visits, one hour = £22.46.

Total cost of case including administration cost (see above): £144.

Example 3

Two offenders had previous convictions. Referred by police, post-arrest. Two victims. Telephoned by scheme and agreed to participate. Offenders received visit at home.

- Preparation time, three hours (£67).

- Conference = one offender, two victims, one member of scheme staff and three unspecified others. Conference lasted one hour and 36 min (£35).

- Outcome – financial compensation to victim, letter of apology to victim (sent).

Total cost of case including administration cost (see above): £224.

Example 4

One previous caution, referred by police post-arrest. Two or more individual meetings with scheme staff, included victim awareness and general offending behaviour.

- One victim- telephoned by scheme. Case appears to have been handled by Inspector. Meetings held at victim's home and offender's home recorded in grid. (£34).

- Preparation time missing, but included two meetings and one phonecall (£8)

- Conference (£34).

Total cost of case including administration cost (see above): £197.

Suffolk County Council (Youth Justice) Caution Plus Scheme

The Caution Plus scheme was based in three YOTs and involved the manager of the respective teams and a co-ordinator who was a police officer in each area and volunteer sessional workers. The panel that referred cases to the scheme was not dependent on the existence of Caution Plus so there was a limit to the degree that cases incurred the costs of assessment of inappropriate cases. However, some cases (estimated between 10 and 15 %) did get a home visit and did not proceed. A home visit was estimated to cost £25. This was inflated to reflect unproductive home visits to £29.

For intervention cases fixed costs included:

* the cost of the panel (£21)
* the cost of the assessment home visit (£29)
* the cost of the initial administration (£4)
* the cost per case associated with training sessional workers (£6)
* the cost of the caution (£20)
* the manager input (£6)
* general co-ordinator activities (£16).

Variable costs include supervision costs, which have been linked to the level of sessional worker input, co-ordinator direct inputs and sessional worker inputs. Supervision costs were based on number of hours spent per week on supervising volunteers and the expected number of weeks that the case would last.

As with Leicestershire, the number of hours spent on the prospective cases (8.4 hours) was much higher than the number of hours estimated to have been spent retrospectively (4.4 hours). Consultation with the area and the researcher suggested that the retrospective estimates were underestimates of the time involved so the total hours input and associated costs were inflated accordingly. The resultant average cost including sessional worker hourly rates to cost volunteers was £244. When actual paid expenses were used the cost per case was just £226.

Appendix D

Additional schemes

The team was asked in April 2000 to review the practices of nine additional schemes. These were:

- Maidstone Mediation Service
- NCH Marvel Reparation Service
- Milton Keynes Retail Theft Initiative
- Northamptonshire Youth Offending Team and Adult Diversion Unit
- Sandwell Mediation Service
- South Yorkshire Victim-Offender Mediation Service
- Thames Valley Restorative Cautioning Project
- *VOCS
- *Walsall Victim-Offender Mediation

*Walsall Victim-Offender Mediation was no longer operating and VOCS could not be contacted.

All the schemes were either visited or substantial documentation was provided. This appendix seeks to describe the work of these projects. All are significantly influenced by the principles of restorative justice with the potential for direct mediation and meeting with victims, except Milton Keynes where a representative victim is used. Of the schemes, two (Northamptonshire and Thames Valley) are large-scale, both with significant resources and would appear to be dealing successfully with large numbers of offenders at their entry point into the criminal justice system. One (Milton Keynes) also deals with entry-level offenders but on a smaller scale and only in relation to retail theft. This specialist approach also appears to be working well. The other four (Maidstone, Marvel, Sandwell, South Yorkshire) are similar in that they are relatively small with limited budgets and staff, dealing with under 100 referrals a year. However they typically take on a broader range of offenders from different points in the criminal justice process. Of these schemes, Marvel and South Yorkshire both appear to be on a solid footing with clear principles and have much to offer from further study.

We now provide a brief description of each scheme in turn.

Maidstone Mediation Service

Maidstone Mediation is an independent charity that trains and supports volunteers to mediate disputes between neighbours and to resolve issues between victims and offenders. The training is all done either in house or with partner agencies. Volunteers receive 25 hours initial training and then do six months' neighbour mediation. There is then a further 25 hours training before victim/offender work is undertaken. There are currently six volunteer mediators. The scheme has been running victim/offender mediation for seven years. They have recently been externally validated by Mediation UK.

The scheme is run by a management committee with representation from social services, probation, the police, Victim Support and local government. There is a half-time paid co-ordinator with some secretarial help. The project is housed in a centre for volunteer agencies. It is funded by local authorities, in particular Maidstone Council with other local authorities and the county council also supplying some funding. The total direct costs for 1998- 99 were £19,456.

Victim/offender work is still supplementary to the scheme's main work in neighbour mediation. It is not a diversion scheme and referrals may come at any point in the criminal justice process if the offender is willing to participate. The reforms in youth justice do not appear to have affected the nature of the scheme's work.

The referral criteria are that the process is voluntary, that the offender admits guilt and that there is an identifiable victim. The referring agency make an initial assessment but the mediators also make an assessment and the case is only progressed if the offender genuinely wishes to take part, admits both the offence and that it was wrong, and that there is no apparent risk to either victim or offender in the process.

Since the beginning of the scheme, there have been 190 referrals of offenders. Thirty pe cent of offenders have no previous convictions or cautions. In 1998, there were 38 referrals from the YOT and two from Victim Liaison, involving 17 offenders between 11 and 15, 21 offenders between 16 and 18 and two offenders over 18. Twenty-six offenders had previous cautions or convictions.

Of the 1998 referrals, 24 involved personal victims and 15 corporate victims. The referring agency usually supplies details of the victim. About 70 per cent of victims are contacted - first by letter or telephone and then a home visit. About 60 per cent of victims take part in some form of mediation.

Offences are mainly acquisitive- burglary, theft, criminal damage and vehicle crime- but the service also dealt with five assaults and three indecent assaults. During their history, there have also been interventions in arson, rape, manslaughter and attempted murder cases.

Of the referrals in 1998, 14 went no further. Nineteen involved indirect mediation, three involved face-to-face mediation and four were still ongoing. The direct mediation usually involved just the offender and the victim- there are very few with family members present. There will be a neutral venue. The normal outcome is an apology and further reparation is rarely negotiated. On average there will be two or three visits for both offender and victim, perhaps three or four phone calls and two or three letters. The process takes about six weeks. Both victims and offenders have registered a high degree of satisfaction with the process

NCH Marvel Reparation Service

This is an independent scheme which concentrates on direct and indirect mediation between victims and offenders. It involves offenders up to 20 years old. It has three centres in North Wales- Shotton in Flintshire, Denbigh and Wrexham- with a full-time worker in each area. The workers are trained by the co-ordinator who runs the Shotton branch and has been deeply involved since its inception.

The scheme was set up in the early 1990s following a detailed review by a multi-agency group. Its philosophy is flexible but ultimately the victim's needs will take priority over those of the offender. Prior to the Crime and Disorder Act 1998, it undertook a wide range of referrals from the pre-caution stage, to interventions following cautions, under supervision and probation orders as well as interventions involving offenders released on licence. At all stages involvement by offenders was voluntary. There is now a new three-year contract with the YOT and Marvel will provide all reparative interventions for the YOT.

The organisation of the scheme is that it is an independent body with three full time workers (one in each centre). The NCH has assumed administrative, budgetary and management responsibilities for the scheme. There is an advisory multi-agency steering committee and a project committee.

The scheme costs £90,000 per annum. Contributions are made from social services, from probation and from NCH. There are other costs; the probation service provides office space and NCH administrative assistance.

The Shotton branch has dealt with 322 cases (as of 7/6/00) in the 5½ years since the start. Of these; approximately 50 were assessed as not suitable. Cases last on average about four to six weeks- the maximum has been nine months. The caseworker thus deals with about 60 cases per year and has about 10 to 12 cases live at any point.

The offender must be under 21 and living in the region. Offences dealt with include property and violent offences- on two occasions, the Shotton branch has dealt with sexual assault but these were wholly exceptional. Before 2000, this was normally at the pre-sentence report stage.

If the victim is identifiable, the caseworker will approach the victim directly. This is not necessarily with mediation in mind as the offender may have been assessed as unsuitable for mediation but to give information and perhaps to seek input on reparation. The needs of the victim are a key factor. The outcome may range from compensation, reparative work of some kind, letters of apology or indirect or direct mediation. Approximately one in 12 cases will involve face-to-face mediation. This may take place in neutral venues such as probation offices, or social services offices. Considerable attention is given to preparing both the victim and offender for such sessions and the caseworker acts as mediator in all cases.

This is a well-organised and successful scheme which is very professional with good records, clear protocols and clear thinking. It publicises its work with posters and leaflets. There is an unpublished evaluation report prepared by North East Wales Institute at Wrexham of which the Home Office has a copy.

Milton Keynes: Retail Theft Initiative

The Retail Theft Initiative has been running for six years and continues largely unaffected by the development of YOTs. The scheme involves first-time shoplifters, employee theft and those handling goods stolen from stores. Offenders attend a programme of interventions on several evenings during which they may meet a proxy victim, a counsellor, a youth worker, a careers' worker, and finish with the administration of a reprimand.

It is run by the police, with input from youth service, other agencies and local stores. Essentially, it is a reintegrative shaming initiative. Referrals are normally juveniles (80%); they attend the scheme with their parent(s). Adults are seen alone although they can bring someone if they wish.

The process begins when an officer is called to a shop where an offender has been detained. Having arrested the offender, the officer makes a PNC check. If a first time offender, and the offence is theft only, he or she is then 'de-arrested' and told that s/he can voluntarily attend the station to be placed on the scheme and receive a restorative caution. If the offence goes beyond theft- e.g. if any criminal damage or assault on the shopkeeper is alleged, including verbal or racial abuse, the case is progressed normally.

The programme commences with a first interview conducted by a police officer. As with the remainder of the programme, this takes place on a Wednesday between 6.00–10.00pm. Adult offenders may bring a friend; all interviews conducted with juveniles require a parent's presence. The offenders are told that their behaviour is unacceptable and that they should think about its consequences. During the interview the officer tries to find the reasons for their offending behaviour. If the offender does not attend this interview, a follow-up call is made. The offender makes an appointment for a future Wednesday event (again usually within two weeks). All arrangements are confirmed by letter. On the second occasion the offender meets:

- a representative from the retail sector (a proxy victim) drawn from a panel, who explains the "ripple" effects of the theft (on the offender, on the parent(s)/immediate family; those who work in the shop, the price of goods in the shop, and thus the cost to those who shop there;

- a counsellor (trained, paid freelance) who talks about 'protective behaviours' (how to deal with peer pressure and bullying);

- a youth worker who explores the offender's family circumstance, schooling, interests and general background;

- two prison officers attend once a month to talk to offenders about what it is really like to be in prison; they show them the clothes that they would wear and the weapons that are made and used by prisoners against each other; and

- a police sergeant or inspector who explains the consequences of offending, and who delivers the formal reprimand with the parent/s present.

Following the reprimand, the offender is usually photographed and fingerprinted.

The scheme's evaluations show that it works. While the programme is entirely voluntary, offender attendance is well over 90 per cent. The co-ordinator estimated that it saves at least four, and usually 5.5, hours' police time per offender compared with the normal processing.

There is in-house training to three levels of their own devising. Level 1 involves awareness of restorative justice activity; level 2 involves developing the ability to deliver a reprimand or caution; level 3 involves developing the ability to mediate.

This is a well organised, adequately resourced programme managed by a highly committed team who have a clear aim and a sense of a mission fulfilled.

Northamptonshire Youth Offending Team and Adult Diversion Unit

This is a statutory multi-agency body which combines an adult and a juvenile diversion unit. For juveniles, it may be described as 'YOT plus'. There is a county management group comprising representatives from the police, youth justice, education, social care and health (formerly social services). The latter currently chairs the group; in the past this has been an ACC. Voluntary groups also have input at this level but not on the ground.

Historically the scheme has sought a balance between concerns about victims and concerns about offenders. The approach to restorative justice interventions may be described as 'eclectic': they choose what works in each particular case. This includes letter writing, direct and indirect mediation, victim empathy and awareness, and other programmes.

There is a pooled budget of £1.6 million. The scheme deals with 1,200 offenders a year comprising 500 adults and 700 juveniles. This figure has fluctuated little since 1993, when two separate provisions for adults and juveniles were combined.

The Diversion Unit (DU) has 20 full-time staff, county wide. There are two teams (one adult, one juvenile), and two location managers, in Northampton and Kettering. All staff are seconded from within the county council employees; they apply for a two or three year secondment. It is a rigorous selection process. Staff generally find the secondment a positive experience. The DU has the final say on who is appointed. There are no volunteers at this level.

The resource manager describes the training as 'significant': offence-focused, with training about victims, protective behaviours, primary and secondary agencies etc. The resource manager himself is a criminal justice committee member of Mediation UK. The training is in-house; there are induction sessions for newcomers, and needs analysis response. Training may also be provided to keep up-to-date, for example with changes in the law.

There are published criteria. Ninety per cent of referrals are pre-court and come from the police. Within the police force there are six 'process markers'. These are administrative employees of the police force who are not necessarily former police officers. They make the referral decisions based on the criteria. They meet regularly as a group, and with the unit managers to discuss cases in general or the operation of the criteria. When they are sent a referral, location managers are formally required to 'receive' it. Although rare, they can send it back for normal processing if they do not think it suitable.

There are forms that are filled in by the process markers which are sent to the location managers. If 'received', staff are then allocated to offenders, according to their skills for the offender in question, for example, if an education issue arises, or the offender is mentally disordered. But basically there is a flexible use of manpower. The teams meet twice weekly to allocate offenders, typically only to one person. Two may be involved if the case is difficult.

Once the offender has been referred and received, that is the end of formal proceedings, whatever the outcome of the intervention.

Initial contact with offenders is by letter; 60 per cent give a positive response (typically 720 cases per annum). Then the victim is contacted. If the victim wants to go ahead, staff act as negotiators to agree an outcome. Most cases are completed by indirect mediation. There is a high level of satisfaction among offenders and victims.

Maintaining the adult work has become difficult now that there are statutory duties for the juveniles. YOT business takes priority and marginal spending decisions go against adult provision. The group is reviewing adult inclusion criteria.

This is a well-managed and well-founded organisation, which is very professional, with good records, clear protocols and clear thinking. Background papers give a lot of detail on the history and on the referral criteria (for adults and the matrix for juveniles). The scheme is being researched by the Institute of Criminology, Cambridge. An evaluative report prepared by Nene College was superseded by one published later by NACRO: *Diverting People from Crime* (June 1998 ISBN 0 85069 147 8).

Sandwell Mediation Service

Sandwell Mediation is a voluntary organisation which has been in existence since 1985 and has held Mediation UK accreditation since 1994. It has close links to Victim Support. A probation officer was seconded to the service in 1992. In 1995 a part-time mediator was appointed, followed in 1996 by a youth justice mediator funded by Sandwell Safer Cities. The total staff now comprises a manager/mediator, a part-time administration manager (also trained as a mediator) and a part-time victim/offender mediator (24 hours per week). The project is housed in a centre for volunteer agencies, but does not use volunteers for mediation work. It provides a comprehensive victim/offender contact service in addition to mediation services in other areas.

Local authorities and the probation service mainly fund the scheme. The total income for 1999-2000 was approximately £76,000, but only about a quarter of this was expended on victim/offender mediation. It is run by a management committee with representation from social services, the police, Victim Support, local government and the tenants' and residents' federation.

Referrals are accepted from victims, offenders, statutory and voluntary agencies, but about 70 per cent of victim/offender referrals come from the probation service. A joint project is run with Brinsford YOI, enabling inmates to be referred to the service for mediation. The referral criteria are that the process is voluntary, that the offender admits guilt, that the offence is not racially motivated and that referrals involving sexual offences are only accepted from the victim.

The scheme has a target of 100 referrals per annum. In 1999- 2000 it received 72. Thirty-six per cent of these involved violent crime (mainly robbery) and 32 per cent burglary. Only one third of these were progressed to mediation (though a further 14% were still live), the main reason for cessation being refusals of victims. Among completed cases, only one resulted in face-to-face mediation. The great majority (83%) was settled by what the scheme calls 'exchanges of information' or 'shuttle diplomacy'. This reflects its philosophy, whereby a key function of mediation is seen to be 'answering victims' questions'. It was stated that nearly all the mediated cases involved several visits carrying messages between victim and offender.

The main problems experienced by the scheme were (a) insecurity of funding (funding was secure for only a year at a time) and (b) difficulties in obtaining victims' details from the police, who have concerns about data protection.

Despite the fact that many referrals are pre-court (and may therefore attract some offenders hoping to gain a reduction in sentence), relatively few 'drop-outs' by offenders were experienced. Most of the drop-outs, in fact, involved offenders on CSO. The manager suggested that it would be productive for probation to allocate some CSO hours officially to mediation to reduce this problem.

Finally, no evaluation of the effectiveness of this scheme has as yet been undertaken.

South Yorkshire Victim-Offender Mediation Service

This service is well-established and has been taking referrals since May 1996 although South Yorkshire probation were running a pilot scheme in the 1980s and were the main instigators of the present project. There is an independent management committee with members drawn from the magistracy, police, media, business, legal profession, Victim Support and Youth Justice. Funding was obtained from the police, the Safer Cities Programme and other sources. The service is now contracted to take referrals from the YOT.

Initially there were two part-time paid co-ordinators and 15 trained volunteers. Since 1996 some 40 volunteers have been trained. The project is not a diversion scheme- although the criteria for referral are broad, they are directed at cases where there has been some sort of formal criminal justice procedure and an admission or finding of guilt. Many offenders have already been cautioned or sentenced. It was rapidly expanded to cover the city of Sheffield and now South Yorkshire.

Between the start and December 1998, there were 183 referrals, not including those from YOT. The demand has been growing with most referrals now coming from the probation service. Most referrals are now at the stage when court proceedings have been commenced or completed. The average period of time between the offence and the referral is 11 months.

The scheme has not addressed itself to 'entry-level' offences. Between July and December 1998, just fewer than 50 per cent of referrals involved theft, burglary or vehicle crime. Over a quarter involved violence and 28 per cent involved robbery. In that period, 60 per cent of victims were female with the average age being 39. But this profile has altered over the existence of the project. Offenders were predominantly young males.

Over the life of the project 30 per cent of completed referrals (47 out of 155) had resulted in some form of mediation and 15 per cent of these were direct mediation. There appears to be a recent trend towards a higher proportion of mediations.

Reports on the service have been written by Iain Crow, Department of Law, University of Sheffield. His evaluation of the scheme was presented to the British Criminology Conference in 1999. He compared a group of mediated offenders with a non-mediated one. Taking into account the kind of offending and the offenders' background, he concluded that while they were based on small numbers, the results indicated that the scheme was heading in the right direction.

Thames Valley Restorative Justice Project

The Thames Valley project is the major initiative in restorative justice in the UK. It was developed and is run by the Thames Valley police force, which covers three counties and is the largest non-metropolitan force. It became operational across the force in April 1998 for juvenile offenders. The following is a basic description of the project.

There is an overall steering group, the Restorative Justice Development Group, which features senior representatives from criminal justice agencies in the force area. The project is co-ordinated by the Restorative Justice Consultancy, a small team of five police staff who also oversees other restorative justice developments within the Force area. Each police area has a dedicated full-time co-ordinator and a number of police officers (from four to 20) who facilitate conferences alongside their normal operational roles. Training is offered to level 3: facilitation of instant cautions; level 2: facilitation of indirect mediation (restorative cautions) and level 1: facilitation of direct mediation (restorative conferences or community conferences).

Several hundred officers have been trained and there is an impressive training manual, originally written in 1997 by Terry O'Connell of the New South Wales police and updated in 1999. It is intended that facilitators will work to the performance criteria set by Level 4 NVQ in Mediation. Force officers put on training for other agencies nationwide.

All first (and some second) time offenders, both adult and juvenile, who fit the criteria for a caution or reprimand, are subject to the programme. This means that there must be sufficient evidence of guilt to give a realistic prospect of conviction, that the offender admits the offence and that the offender understands the significance of the caution.

In the last year approximately 5,000 cases were dealt with, 75 per cent of whom were males between the ages of 16 and 24. Of these, 4,200 are dealt with by indirect, and 800 by direct, mediation.

Although on arrest an 'instant' caution is available, this is not a preferred option. Instead, upon receipt from the arresting officer, a facilitator contacts the offender and arranges (usually) a home visit- with parents present where the offender is a juvenile. There are three types of mediation: "restorative conferencing" comprising the victim, the offender and the offender's family; "community conferencing" in which a community representative is also present; and "restorative cautions", in which there is no victim or community representative present, and a police officer delivers a police caution in a restorative style to the offender in the presence of his or her family.

The scheme is currently being piloted for three years and is being evaluated during this time by the Oxford Centre for Criminological Research. This evaluation will be complete in spring 2001 although interim reports have been produced.

Appendix E

Consent letters

Two consent letters were used: one to be sent to potential victim and offender interviewees (contact letter), the second recording consent to interview (interview consent letter).

Contact letter

The *[name of scheme]* is currently co-operating with a national research project which is studying our work with *[victims and offenders/ young people]*. Six other schemes around the country are also co-operating with the work. We think this is a very important study and hope you will be able to take part.

Enclosed with this letter is a short description of the research project and its main aims. As you will see, the research team are very keen to hear the views of people who have participated in this scheme's work. A person from the research team may wish to speak to you in complete confidence at some point during your involvement with us. The interviews will be fairly short and confidential. You will not be identified by the researchers in anything they write.

You are not obliged to take part. If you DO NOT want to be contacted by the researcher, please complete the tear-off strip below and return it in the pre-paid envelope as soon as possible.

If we do not hear from you, we will assume that you do not mind being contacted by the researcher. When they contact you they will ask if you would be willing to help – you can still refuse – and they will explain the study in more detail.

Thank you for your help.

THE VICTIM AND OFFENDER RESEARCH PROJECT

I do not wish to be contacted in connection with the above research project:

Name: _____ (print)

Signed :_____ Date: _____

Interview consent letter

THE VICTIM AND OFFENDER RESEARCH PROJECT

We are currently conducting an important study for the Home Office of people's experiences of victim and offender schemes. We would like you to help us by taking part in this study.

With your agreement, we would like to interview you. The interview will take about half an hour and will seek your views about the way in which your recent case was handled. The researcher will arrange to do the interview with you at a time most convenient for you.

Anything you say to the researcher will be completely confidential. You will not be identified in anything we write and we will not tell anyone what you have said. *[OFFENDERS] If you are selected to be interviewed and agree to take part in the study we will give you a £10 voucher to compensate you for your time.

If you have any questions about the study please ask the researcher who will be happy to answer them.

This research has been explained to me. I agree to take part.

SIGNED: _____(Participant)

SIGNED: _____(Researcher)

Where appropriate for a parent/guardian to give permission:

I give my permission for _____ to take part in this research study.

SIGNED: _____

Retrospective data record grid

VICTIM AND OFFENDER RESEARCH PROJECT
Retrospective Data Record Grid

[ENTER MISSING OR UNAVAILABLE DATA AS "-9"
Where quantity responses are estimated suffix "E" to the numerical entry]

Project client I.D No. ☐☐☐   PNC Number ☐☐☐☐☐☐☐☐

Local scheme I.D No. ☐☐☐☐   CRO Number ☐☐☐☐☐

Offender's Details:

1. Date of Birth: ☐☐☐☐☐☐ (DD/MM/YY)

2. Age at the date of referral to the scheme: ☐☐ years

3. Gender: Male ☐ Female ☐

4. Ethnic origin: (tick one box)

White British ☐ White European ☐ White Unspecified ☐

White Other (specify) _____

Black Caribbean ☐ Black African ☐ Black Unspecified lack ☐

Other (specify) _____

Black British ☐ Pakistani ☐ Bangladeshi ☐ Indian ☐

Asian Other (specify) _____

Chinese ☐ Mixed race ☐ Unknown ☐ Other (specify) _____

5. Occupational status at the time of referral to the scheme: (tick one box)

In work ☐ Unemployed ☐ In education ☐ Excluded from school ☐

In custody ☐ Other (specify) _____ Don't know ☐

6. Current Primary offence (enter a "1" in the box for primary offence; enter a "2" in the box for secondary offence if the secondary offence led to referral to the scheme).

Theft of car ☐ Theft from car ☐ TWOC ☐ Theft/Handling ☐

Shoplifting ☐ Burglary ☐ Criminal Damage ☐ Common Assault ☐

ABH (s.47) ☐ GBH (s.18/20) ☐ Homicide ☐ Attempted Homicide ☐

Robbery (incl. mugging and snatch theft) ☐ Arson ☐ Sexual offence ☐

DDD ☐ Fraud ☐ Other (specify) ——————————————— Not known ☐

7. What was the date of sentence/caution for the current primary offence? (enter date or tick one of the alternative boxes)

☐☐☐☐☐☐ (DD/MM/YY)

Date unknown ☐ N/A (no court appearance) ☐ Cautioned ☐

8. What was the sentence for the primary offence? (tick one box)

Discharge/Bound Over ☐ Fine ☐ Probation Order ☐ Community Service Order ☐

Combination Order ☐ Suspended Sentence ☐ Custody ☐ Supervision Order ☐

Other ——————————————— (specify) Don't know ☐ N/A Caution ☐

   8a. If "CUSTODY, CSO or Probation Order, how long was the sentence? ☐☐ months.

Not known ☐

9. **Previous offending** (Enter a 'tick' in the first box if "YES" or "-9" if "not known", then indicate the number in the second set of boxes suffixing "E" if the number indicated is an approximation.)

Any previous cautions? ☐ If yes, how many? ☐☐

Any previous guilty appearances? ☐ If yes, how many? ☐☐

Any previous prison sentences ☐ If yes, how many? ☐☐

Any official breaches ☐ If yes, how many? ☐☐

Any custodial sentence when aged u/21 years? ☐   If yes, how many? ☐☐

No previous offending ☐   Don't know ☐

10. Previous offences (tick all that apply, including any for which a "Caution" was given.)

Theft of car ☐ Theft from car ☐ TWOC ☐ Theft/Handling ☐

Shoplifting ☐ Burglary (_____) ☐ Criminal Damage ☐ Common Assault ☐

ABH (s.47) ☐ GBH (s.18/20) ☐ Homicide ☐ Attempted Homicide ☐

Robbery (incl. mugging and snatch theft)   Arson   Sexual offence

DDD ☐ Fraud ☐ Other (specify)——————— Don't know ☐ None ☐

11. Age at first conviction ☐ years. ☐ Don't know ☐ N/A (no prev. conviction) ☐

    11a. Age at first caution ☐ years. ☐ Don't know ☐ N/A (no prev. caution) ☐

12. Has the offender ever been convicted of burglary? YES ☐ NO ☐ Don't know ☐

Referral to the scheme

13. Was this case referred to the scheme? YES ☐ NO ☐

    13a. If YES, by whom? Police ☐ Probation ☐ Social Services ☐ Offender ☐

Victim Support ☐ Local Youth Panel ☐ Other (specify) —————— DK ☐

14. Date of referral (enter "-9" if data is missing): ☐☐☐☐☐☐ (DD/MM/YY)

15. Stage of referral: (tick one box)

Post-arrest ☐ Informal warning ☐ First Reprimand ☐ Caution/FW ☐ PSR ☐

Post-sentence ☐ Don't know ☐

16. Did the scheme assess this case as suitable for intervention?

YES ☐ NO ☐

    16a. How many offenders were involved in this case ☐☐ (number)   N/A ☐

17. Was there any face-to-face contact between the scheme staff and the offender?

YES ☐ NO ☐

    17a. If NO, why not? (tick all that apply) ☐

The type of case (offence) is not dealt with by the scheme ☐

There were safety concerns ☐

There were resource limitations ☐

The offender was not suited to the intervention ☐

The offender was not willing to participate in the scheme ☐

The offender did not plead guilty to the offence ☐

The offender is not living within the local area ☐

The offender could not be contacted by the scheme ☐

The offender re-offended ☐

The victim declined to participate in the intervention ☐

The victim is not living in the local area ☐

The victim could not be contacted by the scheme ☐

The victim did not respond to contact by the scheme ☐

No reason given/Don't know ☐

Other (specify) _____

    17b. If YES, what was the nature of the face-to-face contact? (tick all that apply, answering subsequent questions in each applicable case)

☐ Don't know

☐ Preliminary interview with no further action

i) If YES, why was no further action taken? (tick all that apply) ☐

Offender assessed as unsuited to the scheme ☐

Offender refused to continue or failed to keep the appointment ☐

The offender re-offended before completing the scheme activities ☐

Intervention/activity was completed ☐

Victim related reasons ☐

Don't know ☐

Other (specify) _____

ii) Did the preliminary interview include any victim awareness component?

YES ☐ NO ☐ Don't know ☐

☐ Two or more individual meetings between scheme staff and offender

iii) If YES, did this involve any of the following elements: (tick all that apply)

Anger management ☐ Victim Awareness ☐ Drugs/alcohol education ☐

General Offending Behaviour ☐ Other _____ (specify) DK ☐

☐ Group work

iv) If YES, were any of the following elements involved: (tick all that apply)

Anger management ☐ Victim Awareness ☐ Drugs/alcohol education ☐

General Offending Behaviour ☐ Other _____ (specify) DK ☐

☐ Community Work

☐ Financial compensation to the victim

☐ Direct reparation to the victim (i.e. work for the victim)

☐ Letter of apology or explanation

vi) If YES, was the letter sent? YES ☐ NO ☐ Don't know ☐

☐ Victim- Offender mediation (direct face-to-face)

☐ Victim-Offender mediation (shuttle)

☐ Family Group Conferencing

☐ Referred/ recommended to other services ――――――――――― (specify)

18. Was the offender involved in any other activities which included the following elements? (tick all that apply)

Anger management ☐ Victim Awareness ☐ Drugs/alcohol education ☐

General Offending Behaviour ☐ Other courses ―――――――――― (specify)

Don't know ☐ No ☐

Victim/s

19. How many victims are there in the current case?

20. Types of victim/s (tick all that apply):

Individual ☐ Small Business ☐ Large Business ☐ Council ☐

School ☐ Don't know ☐

Other ―――――――――――――――――――――― (specify)

21. What was the offender's relationship with the victim/s? (tick all that apply)

Partner ☐ Relative ☐ Acquaintance ☐ Friend ☐ Neighbour ☐

Stranger no relationship ☐

Employer ☐ Other _____ (specify)   Don't know ☐

22. Was there contact between the scheme's staff and the victim/s?

YES ☐ NO ☐ Don't know

   22a. If yes, what was the victim/s response to the initial contact? (tick all that apply)

   Accepted ☐   Declined ☐   Didn't reply ☐   Don't know ☐

   22b. How was initial contact made? (tick all that apply)

   Letter from scheme ☐ Telephoned by scheme ☐ Visited by scheme ☐ N/A ☐

   Letter and visit from scheme ☐ Other (specify) _____ Don't know ☐

23). Were there subsequent contacts between the scheme staff and the victim/s?

YES ☐ NO ☐ Don't know

   23a. How were subsequent contacts made? (tick all that apply)

   Letter ☐ Telephone ☐ Visit at home ☐ Visit at scheme ☐ Visit elsewhere ☐

   Other (specify) _____ Don't know ☐ N/A (no contact) ☐

24. Did the scheme offer a victim the opportunity for contact with the offender/s?

YES ☐ NO ☐ Don't know ☐ N/A ☐

Outcome of intervention

25. Was the intervention with the offender completed?   YES ☐ NO ☐

Don't know ☐

25a. If no, why not? (tick all that apply)   ☐

Offender withdrew (intervention incomplete)   ☐

Victim withdrew (intervention incomplete)   ☐

Offender re-offended   ☐

Offender failed to keep appointment/s   ☐

Victim failed to keep appointment/s   ☐

Resource limitations   ☐

Other (specify) _____

Process

26. Complete the following boxes, approximating where necessary. (Suffix "E" to denote approximations. Insert "-9" if information is unavailable or not estimable.)

Leicester and Mansfield

Number of meetings attended:	By Offender	By Victim/s	By scheme Staff	By other (specify)
At scheme Office				
At Participant's Home				
At Other Venue/s				
TOTAL VISITS:				

Activities	By Volunteers	By paid volunteer	By Worker	By Manager	By Non-scheme Staff
Total no. of Hours Spent on Case					
Total Preparation Time on Case					
Total no. of Meetings (any type) attended.					
Total Travel Expenses Claimed					

Gloucester and West Midlands
("E" for estimate. Enter "-9" if information is missing)

	OFFENDER		VICTIM		BOTH	
No of visits	(attempted)	(completed)	(attempted)	(completed)	(attempted)	(completed)
Home						
Other						

Activities	Offender	Victim	Other (specify)
No. of telephone calls			
No of letters written			

West Yorkshire

Number of visits:	Offender/s	Victim/s	Both
At scheme Office			
At Participant's Home			
At Prison			
At Other Venue/s			
Total Number Of Visits:			

Activities	Co-ordinator (manager)	Mediator (sessional)	Mediator (volunteer)	Clerical Assistant
Total no. of Hours Spent on case				
Total no. of letters sent				
Total no. of 'phone calls made and received				
Total no. of assessment reports				
Total no. of meetings				
Total amount of travel expenses claimed				

AMENDS and Suffolk

Suffix "E" to denote approximations. Insert "-9" if information is unavailable or not estimable. Insert "N/A" to denote not applicable.

Number of visits: (Suffix "A" to indicate an attempted visit)	Offender/s	Victim/s	Both
At scheme Office			
At Participant's Home			
At Other Venue/s			
Total Number Of Visits:			

Activities	Co-ordinator	Scheme worker	Volunteer	Other (specify)
Total no. of Hours Spent on Case				
Total no. of letters written				
Total no. of Meetings attended (excluding home visit & Youth Liaison Committee)				
Total Travel Expenses Claimed				

Cost effectiveness ORIGINAL TABLES

Number of visits:	Offender/s	Victim/s	Both
At scheme Office			
At Participant's Home			
At Prison			
At Other Venue/s			
Total Visits:			

Activities	Volunteers	Worker	Manager	Total
Total no. of Hours Spent on case				
Total Travel Expenses Claimed				
Meetings (any type) attended				

Prospective data record grid

Victim and Offender Research Project
Resource use data collection sheet

Project client ID _____ Local scheme ID _____

Start date _____ End date _____

Time inputs from scheme during period of assessment and restorative activities

Activity details	Each activity undertaken										
Activity type (A,T,M,D,S,O)											
Purpose of activity (A,I)											
Location (H,O,P,E)											
Date											
Time spent (minutes – including travel time)											
Scheme staff: Manager (number)											
Worker (number)											
Volunteer (number)											
Others involved in contact:											
Number of victims											
Offender (tick if present. If should have been present but was not, code N)											
SW (grade S or B)											
PO (grade S or B)											
Police (grade I, Sg, PC)											
Other (specify)											

Activity
A   General administration activity (e.g. record keeping)
D   Informal discussions/ meetings
M   Meeting/visit/conference
S   Supervision of restorative activity (e.g. gardening)
T   Telephone conversation
O   Other please specify

Purpose of activity
A   Assessment for suitability for participation in the scheme
I   Implementation of scheme activities

Location
H   Private household (victim or offender)
O   Meeting at scheme office
P   Prison or police station visit
E   Elsewhere please specify

Grade
B   Basic grade
S   Senior
PC   Police constable
Sg   Sergeant
I   Inspector or above

Scheme initiated professional involvement

Type of professional	Grade /pay scale	No. of sessions	Average length of sessions (minutes)	Location of sessions (home/ office/other)	Purpose of activity
Probation					
Police					
Social worker					
Counsellor					
Psychologist					
Educational psychologist					
Educational social worker					
Drug worker					
Other (specify)					

Purpose of activity
Pre or postcode?
AM   Anger management
VA   Victim awareness
D   Drug awareness
Al   Alcohol awareness/education

Scheme initiated group participation

Groups attended	No. participating in group	Group facilitator: SW, PO, Police, Psychologist, Other – please specify	No. of sessions	Length of sessions (minutes)	Location of sessions: home/office /other
Anger management					
Victim awareness					
Drug education/					
Rehabilitation					
Alcohol education/					
Rehabilitation					
Other (specify)					

Ongoing professional involvement (unrelated to intervention)

Type of professional	Number of contacts during period
Probation	
Police	
Social worker	
Counsellor	
Psychologist	
Educational psychologist	
Educational social worker	
Drug worker	
Other (specify)	

Victims questionnaire

Victim and Offender Research Project
Victims' Telephone Interview Schedule

Project client ID No.: ⬚⬚⬚

Local scheme ID No.: ⬚⬚⬚⬚⬚

We are currently conducting an important research project for the Home Office which is looking at people's experiences of [Name of the scheme]. Six other similar schemes around the country are also being studied. An important element of our study is to consider the views and perspectives of people who have been victims and have been in contact with one of the schemes. We are grateful to you for agreeing to help us by taking part in this study.

This interview will take about half an hour. I'm going to be seeking your views about the way in which your recent case was handled and about the details of your involvement with the victim and offender scheme. I will be writing a note of your answers to each question as we go. Anything you say to me will be completely confidential. You will not be identified in anything we write and we will not tell anyone what you have said. Do you have any questions?

Before I start asking you about your involvement with the scheme, I'd like to ask some general background questions about you...

1. Victim's Details

1. Were you directly the victim of a crime or were you representing an organisation which was the victim of a crime?

Individual ⬚ Small business ⬚ Large business ⬚ Council ⬚ School

2. Victim's Gender: Male ⬚ Female ⬚ N/A (organisation) ⬚

3. What age are you? ⬚⬚ years   N/A (organisation) ⬚

4. Please could you tell me how you would describe yourself in terms of ethnic group:

White British ⬚ White European ⬚ White Other (specify) _____

Black British ⬚ Black Caribbean ⬚ Black African ⬚

Black Other (specify) _____

Indian ☐ Pakistani ☐ Bangladeshi ☐ Chinese ☐

Asian Other (specify) _____

Mixed race ☐ Other (specify) _____

2. Offence

5. What sort of crime was committed against you?

Theft of car ☐ Theft from car ☐ TWOC ☐ Theft/Handling ☐

Shoplifting ☐ Burglary (_____) ☐ Criminal Damage ☐ Common Assault ☐

ABH (s.47) ☐ GBH (s.18/20) ☐ Homicide ☐ Attempted Homicide ☐

Robbery (incl..mugging and snatch theft) ☐ Arson ☐ Sexual offence ☐

DDD ☐ Fraud ☐ Other (specify) _____ Not known ☐

5a. Did you think the crime was racially motivated in any way? YES ☐ NO ☐ N/A ☐

6. Please could you indicate which of the following best describes the extent to which you were affected by the crime? **(If NOT an individual victim, this question relates to the effect on the organisation)**

'very much' ☐ 'quite a lot' ☐ 'a little' ☐ 'not at all' ☐

(Ask individual victims only)

7. Did you know the offender before the offence occurred? YES ☐ NO ☐

N/A (organisation)

7a. If yes, in what way?

Partner ☐ Relative ☐ Acquaintance ☐ Friend ☐ Neighbour ☐

Other (specify) _____

8. Were you informed of the outcome of the court case?

YES ☐ NO ☐ N/A (no court case) ☐ N/A (attended court in person) ☐

8a. If yes, by whom _____

(Ask individual victims only)

9. Have you been the victim of a crime before? YES ☐ NO ☐ N/A (organisation) ☐

9a If yes, approximately how many times? ☐☐

9b. If yes, what crime/s were committed against you?

Theft of car ☐ Theft from car ☐ TWOC ☐ Theft/Handling ☐

Shoplifting ☐ Burglary (_____) ☐ Criminal Damage ☐ Common Assault ☐

ABH (s.47) ☐ GBH (s.18/20) ☐ Homicide ☐ Attempted Homicide ☐

Robbery (incl. mugging and snatch theft) ☐ Arson ☐ Sexual offence ☐

DDD ☐ Fraud ☐ Other (specify) Not known ☐

3. Contact with the scheme

Now I'm going to ask you some questions about what happened when you were in contact with the scheme.

10. Who made the initial contact between you and the scheme?

You ☐ Your family/friends ☐ scheme staff ☐ Someone else (specify). ☐

Don't know ☐

10a. How was contact first made?

Telephone ☐ Letter ☐ Visit to your home ☐ Visit to the scheme ☐

Visit to victim organisation ☐ Visit elsewhere ☐ Can't remember/DK ☐

10b. After the initial approach did you need time to make up your mind about whether to get invoved in the scheme?

YES ☐ NO ☐ N/A (no approach) ☐

10c. If yes, about how long was it between first being approached and deciding to participate?

Immediate decision ☐ 1-2 days ☐ 1 week ☐ more than one week ☐

10d. Did the ethnic origin of the scheme representative with whom you were in contact affect your reponse to the scheme?

YES ☐ NO ☐ N/A ☐

11. How many times have you had contact with the scheme by: [indicate the number, suffixing with "E" to denote approximations].

Telephone ☐☐ Letter ☐☐ Visit to your home ☐☐ Visit to the scheme ☐☐

Visit to victim organisation ☐☐ Visit elsewhere ☐☐

12. When contact was made with the scheme, what did they offer you?
(PROMPT: what activities did they discuss with you?)

Activities offered	Tick all that apply	How did the offender describe it?
Money from the offender		
Work by the offender		
Letter of apology/explanation		
Victim-Offender Mediation (face-to-face)		
Victim-Offender Mediation (shuttle)		
Family Group Conference		
Information		
The opportunity to express views		
The opportunity to help the offender		
OTHER (support?…)		

12a. How did you feel about what was offered?
(PROMPT: Did you accept or decline what was offered? Why did you do so?)

Activities offered	Tick all that apply	How did the offender describe it?
Money from the offender		
Work by the offender		
Letter of apology/explanation		
Victim-Offender Mediation (face-to-face)		
Victim-Offender Mediation (shuttle)		
Family Group Conference		
Information		
Opportunity for the victim to express his/her views		
Opportunity to help the offender		
OTHER…		

13. What happened as a result of this contact? Please can you describe what happened?
[PROMPT: How did you become involved? What did you have to do? Who else was involved?]
13a. How did you feel about it?

Activities offered	Tick all that apply	How did the offender describe it?
Money from the offender		
Work by the offender		
Letter of apology/explanation		
Victim-Offender Mediation (face-to-face)		
Victim-Offender Mediation (shuttle)		
Family Group Conference		
Information		
Opportunity for the victim to express his/her views		
Opportunity to help the offender		
OTHER...		

13a. How did you feel about it?

Activities	Tick all mentioned	How did the victim describe it?
Money from the offender		
Work by the offender		
Letter of apology/explanation		
Victim-Offender Mediation (face-to-face)		
Victim-Offender Mediation (shuttle)		
Family Group Conference		
Information		
Opportunity for the victim to express his/her views		
Opportunity to help the offender		
OTHER...		

4. Impact of Involvement

14. Did anything that happened alter your views of the offender?   YES ☐ NO ☐

    14a. If YES, what changed your views and how were they changed?

    14b. If NO, please explain.

15. Do you think what happened had any impact on the offender? YES ☐ NO ☐

15a. If YES, what do you think had an effect and how?

15b. If NO, why not?

Now I am going to ask you about what you thought about the activities that you took part in or your contact with the scheme in general. I will read out a series of short statements and for each I would like you to tell me which of the following best describes your feelings: "All of the time", "Most of the time", "A little of the time" or "None of the time".

16. I understood what was going on.

    ☐ All of the time

    ☐ Most of the time

    ☐ A little of the time

    ☐ None of the time

17. I didn't get to have my say.

☐ All of the time

☐ Most of the time

☐ A little of the time

☐ None of the time

18. I was not listened to.

☐ All of the time

☐ Most of the time

☐ A little of the time

☐ None of the time

19. People seemed to understand my side of things.

☐ All of the time

☐ Most of the time

☐ A little of the time

☐ None of the time

20. I was pushed into things.

☐ All of the time

☐ Most of the time

☐ A little of the time

☐ None of the time

21. I was treated with respect.

☐ All of the time

☐ Most of the time

☐ A little of the time

☐ None of the time

21a. If answer all of the time/most of the time, how were you shown respect?

21b. If answer a little of the time/ none of the time, please explain

5. General impressions

22. Which aspect of your involvement with the scheme was the most positive for you?

23. Which aspect of your involvement with the scheme was the most negative for you?

24. What was the overall effect on you of your involvement with the scheme?

(Ask individual victims only)

25. What was the overall effect on others in your household of your involvement with the scheme?

26. Did contact with the scheme alter your views of the criminal justice system?

YES ☐ NO ☐

    26a. If yes, in what ways?

    26b. If no, please explain.

27. Do you feel the offender has made amends for what he/she did? YES ☐ NO ☐
[PROMPT: Has he/she made up for what he/she did]?

28. What is your general impression of the scheme's work?
(PROMPT: Would you recommend involvement to others who found themselves in a similar position to you? Would you get involved again? In what ways and why?)

29. Overall, in relation to your involvement with the scheme, would you say you were:

Very Satisfied ☐ Satisfied ☐ Neither Satisfied ☐ Dissatisfied ☐ Very Dissatisfied
                                    nor Dissatisfied

30. Were you contacted by any other agency in connection with the offence, other than the scheme?

Police ☐ Victim Support ☐ Other _____ (specify)

6. Preferences/Recommendations

31. Was there anything else you would like to have happened?

Activities offered	Tick all that apply	How did the offender describe it?
Preliminary interview with scheme worker		
Two or more individual meetings with scheme worker		
Group work		
Referred on elsewhere for individual or group work [PROMPT: what type/s of activity was offered?(e.g. Anger management; Victim awareness; Drug/alcohol education; General offending/Cognitive skills course; Counselling)		
Work for the victim		
Money for the victim		
Work for the community		
Letter of apology/explanation		
Victim-Offender Mediation (shuttle)		
Victim-Offender Mediation (face-to-face)		
Family Group Conference		
OTHER...		

32. How might the process be improved, if at all, for victims in the future?

THANK YOU VERY MUCH FOR TAKING PART.

Offenders questionnaire

VICTIM AND OFFENDER RESEARCH PROJECT
Offenders' Interview Schedule

Project client ID No.: ☐☐☐

Local scheme ID No.: ☐☐☐☐☐

We are currently conducting an important research project for the Home Office which is looking at people's experiences of [Name of the scheme]. Six other similar schemes around the country are also being studied. An important element of our study is to consider the views and perspectives of people who have offended and have been in contact with one of the schemes. We are grateful to you for agreeing to help us by taking part in this study.

This interview will take about half an hour. I am going to be seeking your views about your involvement with [Name of the scheme]. I will be writing a note of your answers to each question as we go. Anything you say to me will be completely confidential. You will not be identified in anything we write and we will not tell anyone what you have said. Do you have any questions?

Before I start asking you about your involvement with the scheme, I'd like to ask some general background questions about you…

1. Offender's Details

1. Offender's Gender: Male ☐ Female ☐

2. How old are you?

3. Please could you tell me how you would describe yourself in terms of ethnic group

White British ☐ White European ☐ White Other (specify) _____

Black Caribbean ☐ Black African ☐ Black Other (specify) _____

Black British ☐ Indian ☐ Pakistani ☐ Bangladeshi ☐ Chinese ☐

Asian Other (specify) _____ Mixed race ☐ Other (specify) _____

2. Offence

4. What offence/s did you commit to bring you in contact with the scheme?
[Tick all that apply]

Theft of car ☐   Theft from car ☐   TWOC ☐   Theft/Handling ☐

Shoplifting ☐   Burglary (_____) ☐   Criminal Damage ☐   Common Assault ☐

ABH (s.47) ☐   GBH (s.18/20) ☐   Homicide ☐   Attempted Homicide ☐

Robbery (incl. mugging and snatch theft) ☐   Arson ☐   Sexual offence ☐

DDD ☐   Fraud ☐   Other (specify) _____ Not known ☐

5. Did you receive a caution for this offence?   YES ☐   NO ☐

   5a. If NO, did you appear in court?   YES ☐   NO ☐

   If offender appeared in court ask…

   5b. What was the sentence you were given?

   Discharge/Bound Over ☐   Fine ☐   Probation Order ☐   Community Service Order ☐

   Combination Order ☐   Suspended Sentence ☐   Custody ☐   Supervision Order ☐

   Other (specify _____ Don't Know ☐

   5c. Was this the first time you have appeared in court?   YES ☐   NO ☐

6. Who or what was the victim?

Partner ☐   Relative ☐   Friend ☐   Neighbour ☐

Acquaintance ☐   School ☐   Council ☐   Small business ☐

Large business ☐   Employer ☐   Other (specify) _____

If victim was an individual ask

   6a. Did you know the victim?   YES ☐   NO ☐

3.Contact with the scheme

Now I am going to ask you some questions about what happened when you were in contact with the scheme.

7. Who told you about the scheme?

Social Worker ☐ Probation Officer ☐ Police ☐ Court ☐

Prison ☐ scheme ☐ YOT ☐ Other (specify) _____

8. When contact was made with the scheme, what did they offer you?

[PROMPT: What type of contact or activities did they discuss with you?]

Activities offered	How did the offender describe his/her feelings about it?
Preliminary interview with scheme worker	
Two or more individual meetings with scheme worker	
Group work	
Referred on elsewhere for individual or group work	
Work for the victim	
Money for the victim	
Work for the community	
Letter of apology/explanation	
Victim-Offender Mediation (shuttle)	
Victim-Offender Mediation (face-to-face)	
Family Group Conference	
OTHER…	

8a. How did you feel about what was offered?
[PROMPT: Did you accept or decline what was offered? Why did you do so? Why did you decide to get involved with the scheme?]

Activities offered	How did the offender describe what happened?
Preliminary interview with scheme worker [PROMPT: did this include victim awareness work?]	
Two or more individual meetings with scheme worker [PROMPT: did this include victim awareness work?]	
Group work [PROMPT: did this include victim awareness work?]	
Referred on elsewhere for individual or group work [PROMPT: what type/s of activity did you do?(e.g. Anger management; Victim awareness; Drug/alcohol education; General offending/Cognitive skills course; Counselling) Who was it run by?]	
Work for the victim	
Money for the victim	
Work for the community	
Letter of apology/explanation	
Victim-Offender Mediation (shuttle)	
Victim-Offender Mediation (face-to-face)	
Family Group Conference [PROMPT: did the victim attend?]	
OTHER...	

9. What happened as a result of this contact? Please can you describe what happened? [PROMPT: How did you become involved? What did you have to do? Who else was involved? How many times did you meet with a scheme worker? Where did the activities take place?]

Activities offered	How did the offender describe his/her feelings about it?
Preliminary interview with scheme worker	
Two or more individual meetings with scheme worker	
Group work	
Referred on elsewhere for individual or group work	
Work for the victim	
Money for the victim	
Work for the community	
Letter of apology/explanation [PROMPT: If taken part in indirect mediation and appeared in court, then ask... How did the mediation experience compare with appearing in court?]	
Victim-Offender Mediation (shuttle) [PROMPT: If taken part in shuttle mediation and appeared in court, then ask... How did the mediation experience compare with appearing in court?]	
Victim-Offender Mediation (face-to-face) [PROMPT: If taken part in direct mediation and appeared in court, then ask... How did the mediation experience compare with appearing in court?]	
Family Group Conference [PROMPT: If taken part in FGC and appeared in court, then ask... How did the conference experience compare with appearing in court?]	
OTHER...	

9a. How did you feel about it?

Activities	Tick all mentioned	How did the offender describe it?
Preliminary interview with scheme worker		
Two or more individual meetings with scheme worker		
Group work		
Referred on elsewhere for individual or group work Work for the victim		
Money for the victim		
Work for the community		
Letter of apology/explanation		
Victim-Offender Mediation (shuttle)		
Victim-Offender Mediation (face-to-face)		
Family Group Conference		
OTHER…		

4. Impact of Involvement

You have just told me that you took part in [contact with scheme or activities the offender discussed]. Now I am going to ask you what you thought about your contact with the scheme in general or the activities you took part in.

[PROMPT: IF OFFENDER HAS TAKEN PART IN COURSES/ACTIVITIES OUTSIDE OF THE SCHEME, CLARIFY THAT YOU WANT THEM TO TRY AND FOCUS ONLY ON ACTIVITIES RUN BY THE SCHEME].

Now I will read out a series of short statements and for each I would like you to tell me which of the following best describes your feelings: "All of the tim"", "Most of the time", "A little of the time" or "None of the time".

10. I understood what was going on.

☐ All of the time

☐ Most of the time

☐ A little of the time

☐ None of the time

11. I got to have my say.

☐ All of the time

☐ Most of the time

☐ A little of the time

☐ None of the time

12. I was listened to.

☐ All of the time

☐ Most of the time

☐ A little of the time

☐ None of the time

13. People seemed to understand my side of things.

☐ All of the time

☐ Most of the time

☐ A little of the time

☐ None of the time

14. I was pushed into things.

☐ All of the time

☐ Most of the time

☐ A little of the time

☐ None of the time

15. I was treated with respect.

☐ All of the time

☐ Most of the time

☐ A little of the time

☐ None of the time

15a. If answer all of the time/most of the time, how were you shown respect?

15b. If answer a little of the time/ none of the time, please explain.

16. Thinking about your contact with the scheme or the activities run by the scheme would say that, overall I thought that what happened to me was fair.

☐ All of the time

☐ Most of the time

☐ A little of the time

☐ None of the time

  16a. Could you tell me more about this?

In this next section, which of the following short statements best describes your feelings: "Strongly agree", "Agree", "Disagree" or "Strongly disagree".

17. Taking part in the scheme helped me to understand that what I did was wrong.

☐ Strongly agree

☐ Agree

☐ Disagree

☐ Strongly disagree

  17a. Could you tell me more about this?

18. Taking part in the scheme helped me to understand that what I do affects other people.

☐ Strongly agree

☐ Agree

☐ Disagree

☐ Strongly disagree

18a. Could you tell me more about this?

19. Taking part in the scheme was worse than I expected.

☐ Strongly agree

☐ Agree

☐ Disagree

☐ Strongly disagree

19a. If agree/strongly agree, why?

19b. If disagree/strongly disagree, why?

20. I have decided to keep out of trouble in the future.

☐ Strongly agree

☐ Agree

☐ Disagree

☐ Strongly disagree

20a. Why do you say that?
[PROMPT: What has affected you most? Do you think that the scheme has had any affect?]

5.Face-to-face meeting with victim and offender (Go to Section 6 if offender did not meet the victim in person)

I would now like to ask you how you felt when you met with the victim. Which of the following short statements best describes your feelings: "Strongly agree", "Agree", "Disagree" or "Strongly disagree".

21. I did not know what to expect before I met the victim.

☐ Strongly agree

☐ Agree

☐ Disagree

☐ Strongly disagree

    21a. If agree/strongly agree, why?

    21b. If disagree/strongly disagree, why?

22. It was helpful to meet the victim.

☐ Strongly agree

☐ Agree

☐ Disagree

☐ Strongly disagree

    22a. If agree/strongly agree, why?

    22b. If disagree/strongly disagree, why?

23. I wanted to tell the victim what happened.

☐ Strongly agree

☐ Agree

☐ Disagree

☐ Strongly disagree

23a. If agree/strongly agree, why?

23b. If disagree/strongly disagree, why?

24. I understand how the victim felt better now than I did before.

☐ Strongly agree

☐ Agree

☐ Disagree

☐ Strongly disagree

25. I think that I showed the victim I was sorry.

☐ Strongly agree

☐ Agree

☐ Disagree

☐ Strongly disagree

26. The victim did not seem to understand my side of things.

☐ Strongly agree

☐ Agree

☐ Disagree

☐ Strongly disagree

27. I feel better after having met the victim.

☐ Strongly agree

☐ Agree

☐ Disagree

☐ Strongly disagree

    27a. If agree/strongly agree, why?

    27b. If disagree/strongly disagree, why?

28. Looking back, I would still choose to meet the victim.

☐ Strongly agree

☐ Agree

☐ Disagree

☐ Strongly disagree

    28a. If agree/strongly agree, why?

    28b. If disagree/strongly disagree, why?

6. General Impressions

29. What do you think the scheme was all about?

30. Which one aspect of your involvement with the scheme was the most positive for you?

31. Which one aspect of your involvement with the scheme was the most negative for you?

32. What was the overall effect on you of your involvement with the scheme?

33. Who do you live with?

Parents ☐   Foster parents ☐   Partner ☐   Friends ☐

Children's Home ☐   Hostel ☐   Alone ☐

Other (specify) _____

34. Did taking part in the scheme affect those you live with or those close to you?
(Note there may be offenders who live alone or feel that they are not close to anyone)
[PROMPT: Who was affected and how? Did anyone close to you support you? Who and in what ways? What was their attitude? How did you feel about what they did and their attitude? (i.e. the presence or absence of support)

7. Preferences/Recommendations

35. Was there anything else you would like to have happened? [PROMPT: use examples of contact and activities from this grid.]

Activities	Tick all mentioned	How did the offender describe it?
Preliminary interview with scheme worker		
Two or more individual meetings with scheme worker		
Group work		
Referred on elsewhere for individual or group work Work for the victim		
Money for the victim		
Work for the community		
Letter of apology/explanation		
Victim-Offender Mediation (shuttle)		
Victim-Offender Mediation (face-to-face)		
Family Group Conference		
OTHER…		

36. If friends of yours got into trouble, would you recommend that they took part in the scheme?

37. How might the scheme be improved, if at all, for offenders in the future?

THANK YOU VERY MUCH FOR TAKING PART.

Scheme staff questionnaire
VICTIM AND OFFENDER RESEARCH PROJECT
Scheme Staff Interview Schedule

Background

1. What did you do before you became involved in the scheme's work?

2. What motivated you to become involved in the scheme's work?

Training

3. Did you receive any training specific to your role in the scheme? If so, what did this involve? (PROMPT: duration and content of training? Who presented the training?)

4. Would you benefit from further training? If so, what?

Scheme

5. What would you say the scheme is trying to achieve?

6. What do you think distinguishes this scheme from other projects which work with offenders?

7. What are your main responsibilities within the scheme?

Work with Victims and Offenders

8. What are your views about the referral criteria for cases? (PROMPT: Are appropriate cases referred? Are others missed who you think would benefit from inclusion?)

9. What are your views about the involvement of victims in the scheme's work? (PROMPT: Could more be done to include them? Could victims be more fully involved? Why does this scheme involve victims in the way that it does?)

10. What do you perceive as the main difficulties of working with victims of crime?

11. Which particular aspects of the scheme's work do you think have the most beneficial impacts or outcomes? For whom? [PROMPT: Particularly for victims and/or offenders]

12. Do you think the scheme's work has any negative impacts or outcomes? For whom?

13. What would you regard as a "successful" case?

14. What would you regard as an "unsuccessful" case?

15. What are the main limitations of the work of the scheme?

Future

16. What are the main lessons you have learned as a result of working in this scheme?

17. In what way/s do you think the scheme's work could be improved upon?

Appendix F   **References**

Allen, C. and Beecham, J. (1993) Costing services: ideals and reality, in A. Netten and J. Beecham (eds) *Costing Community Care: Theory and Practice*. Ashgate, Aldershot.

Baldwin, J. and Bottoms, A.E. (1976) *The Urban Criminal*. London: Tavistock.

Ball, C. (2000) 'The Youth Justice and Criminal Evidence Act 1999: Part 1: A significant move towards restorative justice, or a recipe for unintended consequences?' *Criminal Law Review*, 211-222.

Banks, C. (1999) 'Victims in the village: aspects of restorative justice in Papua New Guinea.' *International Review of Victimology*, 6: 377-405.

Barclay, G. (ed.) (1991) *A Digest of Information on the Criminal Justice System*. London: Home Office.

Bazemore, G. (1998) 'Restorative justice and earned redemption: communities, victims, and offender reintegration.' *American Behavioral Scientist*, 41: 768-813.

Bazemore, G. (1999) 'Crime victims, restorative justice and the juvenile court: exploring victim needs and involvement in the response to youth crime.' *International Review of Victimology*, 6: 295-320.

Bazemore, G. and Walgrave, L. (1999) 'Restorative juvenile justice: in search of fundamentals and an outline for systemic reform.' In Bazemore, G. and Walgrave, L. (eds)., *Restorative Juvenile Justice: Repairing the Harm of Youth Crime*. Monsey NY: Criminal Justice Press.

Braithwaite, J. (1989) *Crime, shame and reintegration*. Cambridge: Cambridge University Press.

Braithwaite, J. (1999) 'Restorative justice: assessing optimistic and pessimistic accounts.' In Tonry, M. (ed.), *Crime and Justice, a Review of Research*, 1-127. Illinois: University of Chicago Press.

Copas, J. and Marshall, P. (1998) 'The offender group reconviction scale: a statistical reconviction score for use by probation officers.' *Journal of the Royal Statistical Society C-App.*, 47: 159-171.

Council of Europe (1999) *Mediation in Penal Matters*. Recommendation No. R(99)19 adopted by the Council of Ministers of the Council of Europe on 15 September 1999.

Crawford, A. and Enterkin, J. (2000) *Victim Contact Work and the Probation Service: A Study of Service Delivery and Impact*. Centre for Criminal Justice Studies, University of Leeds.

Crawford, A. and Goodey, J., (eds.) (2000) *Integrating a Victim Perspective in Criminal Justice*. Abingdon: Ashgate.

Crime Prevention Council in Denmark (1999) *An Experiment with Victim Offender Mediation in Denmark*. Copenhagen; Denmark.

Crow, I. (1999) 'Victim-offender mediation: the experience of the Sheffield scheme.' Paper given at the British Criminology Conference, 1999.

Davis, G., Boucherat, J., and Watson, D. (1988) 'Reparation in the service of diversion: the subordination of a good idea.' *Howard Journal*, 27: 2-00.

Dignan, J. (1999) 'The Crime and Disorder Act and the prospects for restorative justice.' *Criminal Law Review*, 48-00.

Dignan, J. (2000a). *Youth Justice Pilots Evaluation: Interim Report on Reparative Work and Youth Offending Teams*. London: Home Office.

Dignan, J. (2000b) 'Victims, reparation and the pilot YOTs.' *Justice of the Peace*, 164: 296-7.

Elechi, O. (1999) 'Victims under restorative justice systems: the Afikpo (Ehugbo) Nigeria model.' *International Review of Victimology*, 6: 359-376.

Frude, N., Honess, T. and Maguire, M. (1998) *Crimepics II: A Psychometric Tool for Measuring Attitude Change in Probation Clients*, Second Edition. London: M & A.

George C. (1999) '*Victim Support's* perspective on restorative justice.' *Prison Service Journal*, 123: 12-14.

Griffiths, C. (1999) 'The victims of crime and restorative justice: the Canadian experience.' *International Review of Victimology*, 6: 279-294.

Griffiths, C. and Bazemore, G., (eds.) (1999) 'Special issue on restorative justice.' *International Review of Victimology*, 6: 265-416.

Hallam, A. and Netten, A. (2001) 'Calculating the costs of interventions by restorative justice schemes', Discussion Paper 1709, PSSRU, University of Kent at Canterbury, Canterbury.

Harries, R. (1999) *The Cost of Criminal Justice*. Research Findings No. 3. London: Home Office, Research and Statistics Directorate.

Home Office (1997) *No More Excuses – A New Approach to Tackling Youth Crime in England and Wales*. London: Cm 3809.

Hoyle, C., Cape, E., Morgan, R. and Sanders, A. (1998) *Evaluation of the 'One Stop Shop' and Victim Impact Statement Pilot Projects*. London: Home Office Research, Development and Statistics Directorate Report.

Hoyle, C., Morgan, R. and Sanders, A. (1999) *The Victim's Charter: An Evaluation of Pilot Projects*. London: Home Office Research, Development and Statistics Directorate. Research Findings No. 107.

Jackson, P. (ed.) (1998) 'Restorative justice: theory meets practice.' *Western Criminology Review*, 1: 1-140.

Liebmann, M. (1999) 'Restorative justice for families.' *Prison Service Journal*, 123: 14-17.

Linden, R. and Clairmont, D. (1998) Making it Work: *Planning and Evaluating Community Corrections and Healing Projects in Aboriginal Communities*. Solicitor-General of Canada, Aboriginal Corrections Policy Unit, Ottawa; Canada.

Lloyd, C., Mair, G. and Hough, M. (1994) *Explaining reconviction rates: a critical analysis* London: Home Office Research Study No. 130.

Mackie, A. and Burrows, J. (1999) *The Milton Keynes Youth Crime Reduction Project*. Research, Development and Statistics Directorate. Research Findings No. 108. Home Office, London; U.K.

Marshall, T. (1999) *Restorative Justice: An Overview*. London: Home Office.

Mediation UK (1999) *Training Manual in Community Mediation Skills*. Bristol: Mediation UK.

Meier, B. (1998). 'Restorative justice: a new paradigm in criminal law?' *European Journal of Crime, Criminal Law and Criminal Justice*, 6: 125-139.

Morris, A. and Gelsthorpe, L. (2000) 'Something old, something borrowed, something blue, but something new? A comment on the prospects for restorative justice under the Crime and Disorder Act 1998.' *Criminal Law Review*, 18-30.

Morris, A. and Maxwell, G. (2000) 'The practice of family group conferences in New Zealand: assessing the place, potential and pitfalls or restorative justice.' In Crawford, A. and Goodey, J.(eds), *Integrating a Victim Perspective in Criminal Justice*. Abingdon: Ashgate. 207-225.

Netten, A. Dennett, J. and Knight, J. (1999) Unit Costs of Health and Social Care 1999 Personal Social Services Research Unit, University of Kent at Canterbury.

New Zealand Ministry of Justice (1999) *Restorative Justice: the Public Submissions*. Ministry of Justice, Wellington, New Zealand.

Palk, G., Hayes, H. and Prenzler, T. (1998) 'Restorative justice and community conferencing; summary from a pilot study.' *Current Issues in Criminal Justice*, 10: 139-55.

Pollard, C. (1999) 'Restoring the faith.' *Policing Today* 36-38 (March).

Pollard, C. (2000) 'Victims and the criminal justice system: a new vision.' *Criminal Law Review*, 5-17.

Prenzler, T. and Hayes, H. (1999) 'Victim-offender mediation and the gate keeping role of the police.' *International Journal of Police Science and Management*, 2: 17-32.

Presser, L. and Lowenkamp, T. (1999) 'Restorative justice and offender screening.' *Journal of Criminal Justice*, 27: 333-343.

Sanders, A. (1999) *Taking Account of Victims in the Criminal Justice System: a Review of the Literature*. Scottish Office, Central Research Unit Report, Edinburgh; U.K.

Sherman, L., Strang, H. and Barnes, C. (1999) *Experiments in Restorative Policing: Progress Report to the National Police Research Unit*. Law Program, Australian National University, Canberra; Australia.

Taylor, R. (1999) *Predicting Re-convictions for Sexual and Violent Offences Using the Revised Offender Group Reconviction Scale*. London: Home Office RDS Findings 104.

Thames Valley Police (1999) *Restorative Conferencing, Facilitator Training Manual*.

Umbreit, M., Bradshaw, W. and Coates, R. (1999) 'Victims of severe violence meet the offender: restorative justice through dialogue.' *International Review of Victimology*, 6: 321-344.

United Nations (1999) *Draft Declaration of Basic Principles on the use of Restorative Justice Programmes in Criminal Matters.*

Walgrave, L. (2000) 'Extending the victim perspective towards a systemic restorative justice alternative.' In Crawford, A. and Goodey, J. (eds), *Integrating a Victim Perspective in Criminal Justice.* Abingdon: Ashgate, 253-284.

Walker, P. (1999) 'Saying sorry, acting sorry.' *Prison Service Journal,* 123: 19-20.

Wasik, M. (1999) 'Reparation: sentencing and the victim.' *Criminal Law Review 470-479.*

Weitekamp, E. (1999a) 'The paradigm of restorative justice: potentials, possibilities and pitfalls.' In van Dijk, J., von Kaan, R. and Wemmers, J. (eds), *Caring for Crime Victims: Selected Proceedings of the 9th International Symposium on Victimology,* 115-125.

Weitekamp, E. (1999b) 'Research on victim-offender mediation: findings and needs for the future.' European Forum for Victim-Offender Mediation and Restorative Justice, University of Leuven; Belgium.

Wright, M. (1998) 'Restorative justice: from punishment to reconciliation: the role of social workers.' *European Journal of Crime, Criminal Law and Criminal Justice,* 6: 267-281.

Wright, M. (1999) *Restoring Respect for Justice.* Manchester: Waterside Press.

Young, M. (1999) 'Restorative community justice in the United States: a new paradigm.' *International Review of Victimology,* 6: 265-277.

Young, R. (2000) '*Integrating a multi-victim perspective into criminal justice through restorative conferences.*' In Crawford, A. and Goodey, J. (eds). Integrating a Victim Perspective in Criminal Justice. Abingdon: Ashgate, 227-251.

Zellerer, E. (1999) 'Restorative justice and indigenous communities: critical issues in controlling violence against women.' *International Review of Victimology,* 6: 345-358.